Author's Note:

Except where expressly specified, all names in the book are pseudonyms and not the actual names of those referenced in any story. The Defense Office of Prepublication and Security Review (DOPSR) reviewed this book before publication to ensure that no classified or operational information was disclosed—my heartfelt appreciation for their work.

Disclaimer: "The views expressed in this publication are those of the author and do not necessarily reflect the official policy or position of the Department of Defense or the US government." And "The public release clearance of this publication by the Department of Defense does not imply Department of Defense endorsement or factual accuracy of the material.

ISBN: 9798287893767

1st Edition Print 2023.
2nd Edition Print 2025.

Publisher address: wkmar2008@gmail.com
| www.linkedin.com/in/warren-pennicooke

Cover and book design by the Author. The Author's picture is courtesy of the University of Hawaii, Army ROTC Cadre 2010.

To Caitlin

For always seeing the best in me and being
my safe harbor.

Foreword By

David L. Porter. Colonel U.S. Army (Ret.). Author of "Taking Fire!" Memoir of An Aerial Scout in Vietnam

I am honored to write this foreword for Warren Pennicooke's first book.

This is exceptional work on a subject that in the senior military world was either a valued tool or the bane of professional Army officers and Non-Commissioned Officers – the Military decision-making process (MDMP).

The process was initially developed in pre-World War I Germany and refined under the leadership of Prussian Field Marshal von Steuben's General Staff. MDMP was developed and refined in those hands-on battlefield laboratories of Prussian Staff Officers and Non-Commissioned Officers. Those legendary staff members played a pivotal role in the military culture, ultimately dominating much of the world.

MDMP is today interwoven into the military's decision-making procedures and recognized as the standard for arriving at proper military decisions. Pennicooke's exposure began as a participant and later as a disciple as he rose through the ranks.

I have known Warren for about fourteen years. As an Army contractor during those years, he was always ahead of the proverbial power curve. He was thoughtful, innovative, and questioning. I was thankful that he turned his considerable analytical powers toward MDMP. The result of his inquiry into the subject is before you. Knowing a little about what is ahead is instructive without giving too much away in advance.

This is the work of a highly competent professional who has excelled within MDMP for over twenty years. In this work, he critically examines the military's decision-making process. Not a small task. He looks objectively at what he has lived as a Soldier against what he has seen and observed over time, against his special Jamaican-bred credos. Warren skillfully compares the tenets of MDMP to situations he has observed in the civilian world. He reviews those situations and draws essential conclusions. Those who may think MDMP has strictly military applications will see numerous examples from the author's rich experience in this work. He exposes misconceptions and falsehoods while maintaining his objectivity. We all have experienced the wonders of MDMP from numerous perspectives and angles. Good, bad, or indifferent career Army folks generally know MDMP. The author has taken his ruminations about MDMP to a new level and exposed its tenets to all of us. He is atypical because he has taken what we were taught and translated the concepts from a military venue to civilian use.

To my knowledge, this is the first book to approach the subject of MDMP from Warren's perspective. It is unique because he is the author, and his conclusions and discussions are unique. He applies all the powers of his compelling communication tools to his analysis. There are scores of books about this subject, but none like Pennicooke's. It is personal, insightful, and believable.

In 1819, the legendary poet John Keats wrote the poem "**Ode to a Grecian Urn**." Ancient Greek mythology and its Truth-centric philosophy held a unique urn to be sacred, believing it contained all Truth. Pennicooke's book does not claim to provide all truth, but it is a crucial addition to the truth of the Military Decision-Making Process.

Updates and Revisions for the New Edition

Since the first publication of this book, several developments have occurred worth mentioning. First, Boeing has announced a change in its leadership, specifically the appointment of a new Chief Executive Officer. Dave Calhoun stepped down at the end of 2024, and Kelly Ortberg was named his replacement.

It is worth noting that Ortberg's appointment coincided with a broader leadership shakeup at Boeing, as the company grapples with ongoing production issues and regulatory scrutiny, with safety at its core.

Samuel Bankman-Fried was sentenced to 25 years for his massive fraud, a win for the rule of law. Bankman-Fried, better known as SBF, was sentenced to 25 years in prison for his role in the collapse of FTX, a once-promising cryptocurrency exchange.

The hefty sentence handed down last year reflects the severity of Bankman-Fried's crimes. It continues to send a powerful message to other would-be white-collar criminals that such actions will not be tolerated. At the same time, the saga of Bankman-Fried's downfall is indeed a cautionary tale. It serves as a reminder of the importance of holding those in positions of power accountable for their actions, particularly when they abuse their authority for personal gain and at the expense and exclusion of others, a theme that runs throughout the book.

Since 2023, the African continent has experienced numerous conflicts. These conflicts include civil wars between African nations, coups, and separatist movements. Some countries that have experienced the most conflict include Sudan, Burundi, and Burkina Faso.

Additionally, the continent has seen an increase in armed conflicts, resulting in a high number of battle-related deaths and displacements. While some progress has been made in resolving specific disputes, such as the recapture of Bunagana by East African regional forces, the overall situation remains complex and challenging.

I did not discuss the war in Ukraine in the first edition. I naively thought it would be over in months, and as I saw it, the manuscript was already written.

However, since Russia's invasion of Ukraine on February 24, 2022, and despite Ukraine's valiant efforts to defend its sovereignty, the ongoing conflict with Russia remains unresolved. While Ukraine has made some progress in counteroffensives, Russian forces continue to hold roughly 20% of Ukrainian territory as of 2024.

The war has also transformed Ukraine's economic structure and caused significant loss of life, both military and civilian. The situation in Ukraine must serve as a sobering reminder of the devastating impact of war and the importance of resolving conflicts peacefully.

In the Middle East since 2023, they have experienced significant conflict and instability, with the Hamas-led attack on Israel in October of that year sparking a series of interrelated conflicts and heightened tensions in the region. The ensuing Israel-Hamas war, which saw Israel launch a destructive bombing campaign and invade the Gaza Strip, has led to widespread protests and condemnation from the international community.

The war has also had ripple effects on the broader geopolitical landscape, with tensions between Israel and Iran escalating significantly. Some experts in human rights organizations have characterized the conflict as a genocide, and legal proceedings are ongoing in the International Court of Justice and the International Criminal Court.

Historians will have plenty of material to write about regarding Israel, Hamas, Gaza, the temple mosque, and the Palestinian people. They always have.

Despite an ongoing ceasefire, the situation remains volatile, with ongoing violence and human suffering affecting millions of people in the region.

Lastly, the administration responsible for the fiasco that was the withdrawal from Afghanistan is no longer in power, and the new administration has vowed to address world issues diplomatically and early in hopes of not putting American troops at war. The president has also indicated that he does not like the military being used as a social experiment.

Prologue

The military decision-making process is said to have both an art and a science component to it. In the context of the military decision-making process (MDMP), the art aspect refers to the intuitive, subjective, and experience-based factors that influence decision-making. This includes understanding and considering the human component — the people involved, their emotions, motivations, and likely behaviors.

Effective leaders recognize that decision-making is not purely a technical or analytical exercise. They understand that considering the human element is crucial when evaluating potential courses of action, anticipating reactions, and assessing potential consequences.

This involves empathizing with the emotions and perspectives of others, understanding group dynamics, and making judgments based on experience and intuition.

Therefore, the art of decision-making in the military context requires a deep understanding of the people involved, both within one's forces and among allies, adversaries, and civilian populations.

It is a critical aspect of the MDMP that helps ensure decisions are not only tactically sound but also account for the complex human dimensions of warfare.

Table of Contents

Chapter 1

"A Good Plan, Violently Executed Now, Is Better Than a Perfect Plan Next Week."

General George Patton

Setting Conditions: The Military Decision-Making Process and Troop Leading Procedures

Processes and systems have relevance, but are useless and unproductive without human interaction. For this reason, their importance cannot be overstated, regardless of which school of thought you subscribe to. Before we can ask others to do something, we must be at least willing to do that thing ourselves.

That is the predicate on which cohesive teams should be founded. But how do teams arrive at this point?

What is the secret to building a team whose performance exceeds the sum of its disparate members? -who are fundamentally and markedly different yet just as distinct in character and attributes.

The answer is cohesion.

Cohesive teams perform better and stay together longer than non-cohesive teams.[1]

Teams can absorb more demanding tasks, perform with fewer errors, and exceed performance based on linear composites of individual inputs.

This was the first conclusion highlighted by Gerald Goodwin, Nikki Blacksmith, and Meredith Coats in their review of six decades of military-team research. Specifically, they emphasize the importance of cohesion and the benefits that solid teams can provide to an organization.[2]

We must pose several other questions before answering how we develop cohesive teams. How do we develop leaders who have the potential to become team leaders? And what will they look like compared to their parents and grandparents of generations ago?

That depends on whom you ask and in what context they respond. Retired Lieutenant General James Dubik, *Commander of the Multinational Security Transition Command-Iraq*, once wrote, *"Trust and confidence result from how confident soldiers are in themselves, their individual and unit training, their equipment, and their leaders."* In short, leaders today must set those conditions through their actions and decisions. If they are willing to learn, junior leaders will grow from the seeds they planted earlier.

Yet, espousing the benefits and highlighting the talking points needed for cohesive teams and team building is not enough.

They must be predicated on and built on pillars that serve as tools for the team. That is, the team must be the sum of its parts. One fails, and the team fails. As such, the people in the group become focus number one. The remaining two composites of processes and systems can be more seamlessly employed by investing in people.

As will be highlighted later, many corporations, businesses, and governments make errors because they cannot fully understand the fundamental interplay that makes a system work. This is essential. However, leadership builds systems and transforms existing ones—a necessary skill set aggressively sought in today's fast-paced, changing world. With that in mind, let us explore this concept as we look deeper at the first tenet: people.

Evidence shows that when leaders fail at change strategies, they often neglect to recognize, encourage, inspire, and give latitude or autonomy to their teams, hindering their growth. And to their and the organization's demise, stagnation and complacency take effect. Meaningful change is never successful unless the level of complacency is low.[3] That means leaders must motivate and inspire at every opportunity because a high urgency rate helps enormously in completing all the stages of a transformation process.

If stated differently, if the rate of external change increases, then the motivation and energy rate must remain either constant, median, or rationally increased.

Vacuums are created in politics and the military when these changes in strategy result in failures. These lacunas, or empty spaces, have many causes, including ill-advised decision-making and other misaligned inputs that hinder effective decision-making.

For countries with unstable governments and thus unstable militaries, specifically in dealing with combat, the mistake of vacuums created by poor decision-making sadly equates to the loss of lives.

There is an old belief in the United States Army that we can reset you in training, but not in combat. This thinking is not just a feeling.

It is real.

Based on this premise, the military prides itself on its processes, including second-to-none decision-making and input from decision-makers.

The process is about getting the correct answer for the leader and empowering the team to unmask themselves and show their true potential. It enables team members struggling with interpersonal issues to acknowledge and address them. Conversely, it puts on notice those who would choose to spotlight themselves over the team.

The Army uses key developmental positions, or progression benchmarks, to help develop the interpersonal skills necessary to accomplish the mission. Success occurs through collaboration and the influx of different perspectives during the various stages.

This process involves officers and non-commissioned officers, fostering cooperation and leading to individual and group growth. The key is that, in addition to working independently, all participants must collaborate and work as a group at some point; otherwise, they will inherently fail to succeed.

It achieves this by providing and demanding a process in which all team members' inputs are given equal weight, considered, discussed, and questioned by their peers in real time.

Even with remote work, these teammates and the military had to conduct their missions leveraging the internet and approved social media platforms to maintain their readiness edge.

I do not have to tell you this is a real-time transformation, and the military must adapt or be left behind.

And I do not have to elaborate on the costs of being left behind.

Then, what makes the Military Decision-Making Process different from the boardroom?

When you peel back the onion, the typical boardroom process does not differ much contextually from that of the military. However, decisions are sectionalized in the corporate boardroom.

They are part of a three-level system. The first level is strategic, involving decisions that the board must make. The second level is tactical, which requires more input and time to manage. Last, operational decisions are made by management and, as their name implies, drive daily operations. As you may have noticed, this system is designed episodically.

Studies have shown that repeating a process over time makes it more seamless and streamlined.

Therefore, the significant difference between the Military Decision-Making Process and the corporate boardroom is that the boardroom processes are more event-based. They occur only when necessary, such as when launching a new product line. Ramped-up efforts are noticeable during these periods, and planning takes center stage. In the military, the process is constantly occurring.

In that respect, the military is more iterative and focuses on team empowerment rather than specific individual tasks at each stage. Overall, it is more team-oriented. It, too, is purposefully designed and built into military doctrine.

Doctrine, like the MDMP, serves as a guidepost—a *way* of sorts or a recommendation on *how to*.

Consider it this way: the central guidelines of an Army are known as its doctrine, which, to be sound, must be based on the principles of war (to which there are several schools of thought on how many principles exist) and which to be effective, must be resilient enough to accept transformation true to a change in circumstances.

In other words, it requires the input of official and command guidance in setting definitive parameters for each theory. Still, it requires judgment in its application because of those changes in circumstances to which Major-General John *"Boney"* Fuller inferred when he said, *"In its ultimate relationship to human understanding, this central idea or doctrine is only common sense—action adapted to circumstances.*[5]*"*

Within this paradigm, team empowerment is even more effective because it forces them to use multiple communication platforms and judgment, which aligns with Fuller's and my point. But more importantly, two-way communication. It reduces the perceived downside of two-way or other communication, in which feedback may suggest that the leader has an ineffective plan or that in-progress projects or products need reformulation.

Military leaders want their teams to provide information and help them turn it into actionable knowledge through visualization. Said differently, they want people who will give them the *so what?* What about these bits and pieces that make them worthwhile and usable?

Armed with these actionable insights, the leader can then make sound and informed decisions. In doing so, they can ensure assigned tasks are understood, supervised, and conducted, and, more importantly, employ their teams to leverage their capabilities.

The leader is allowed this flexibility to seamlessly complete their tasks because the team reframes the problem with recommendations from the bits and pieces. In other words, they broadened and stretched the problem by applying multiple dilemmas to examine all the variables. This process is time-consuming and deliberate. Like the boardroom's decision-making process, it is also tedious by nature and design. In this internal portion of the process, contingencies and redundancies are discussed and added. Ownership of specific tasks begins to materialize.

If not done this way, leaders risk soldiers getting seriously hurt or, worse yet, dying because the first project or plan fails, which anyone who has served will tell you always happens. *The first plan never survives first contact.* The model requires no, scratch that. It is essential to incorporate contingencies and redundancies into any project to ensure its success.

Consider this example: Suppose Sam launched his product late for reasons that were initially unknown. Indeed, the competition may have beaten him at the top and bottom lines. However, consider if they rushed the product to market to beat Sam. Consider that they are now facing lawsuits due to faulty production. Conversely, assume that Sam utilized and ultimately reaped the benefits of a more robust, deliberate process with the right people in the right places. People properly positioned and

tasked with the right tasks launched a similar product—a better product, not recalled six months later
for a faulty design like the competitors'.

The corporate world, for its part, although it has
improved, still reveres individual accomplishments
over teams, which creates subgroups.

These are not the subgroups in integrated com-
munities that play a crucial role in cultivating inter-
relatedness and exchanging professional and scien-
tific knowledge, but the kind that breeds envious,
self-serving behaviors.

To capitalize on this perceived opportunity,
many teammates view it as a chance to showcase
their individuality. Which, on the surface, is not im-
moral, unethical, or even illegal.

We are witnessing the erosion of the existing culture or, worse yet, the setting of new, lower standards.

The benefits of deliberate leadership, such as putting people at the forefront of a change initiative,
launching a new product, or preparing for combat,
are monumental and ought to be.

Failure here has considerable implications in an
ever-transforming world. I am no fan of cliches.
However, the cliché' *failure is not an option* seems
prudent here. That makes the positioning of people
the driving force behind the success of the decision-
making process.

As such, this concept and skill of having the right
people at the points of friction alleviate single
points of failure. In the private and public sectors,
this is often the result of a single person behaving
criminally and is not usually associated with the
company's core culture.

In the military, where the opposite is often accurate, and the culture is built around leadership at all levels, unchecked single points of failure can become ingrained in the culture. This can have very problematic outcomes regarding readiness.

A more significant point is that, by definition, a single point of failure in any context can lead to the demise of the entire system; therefore, alleviating its impact on your culture is paramount.

And yet, in all things people-centric, there will be anomalies. Anomalies in this context consider all the properties of the human psyche. Psychologist Carl Jung [6] famously described it this way, *"By psyche, I understand the totality of all psychic processes, conscious as well as unconscious."*

Then, his thinking, as well as that of anyone using the reasonable person standard, removes any notion that the Military Decision-Making Process is a panacea. However, the Military Decision-Making Process, if not the gold standard, should be considered in that conversation. It places the correct principles in the right environment, along with the right strategies and systems, to solve challenging problems.

Its iterative planning method forces and facilitates collaboration, building a shared understanding across all sections and departments. This is achieved through active participation in the development of courses of action and conflict resolution before disseminating the final plan across the enterprise.

It is not a knee-jerk reactionary process. It can be used deliberately and, where and when appropriate, abbreviated, such as in combat. Or, as I said earlier, immediately during a crisis on the hoods of tactical and first responder vehicles.

However, the basic principles that drive the process are not lost when it is shortened. At worst, time and space are its Achilles' heel.

Liaisons bridge communication gaps caused by time and space. We will soon discuss them and their significance. Until then, we can agree that leadership is a process whereby an individual influences a group to achieve a common goal, where affecting people is at the core. It is equally plausible to assert that the solution to business transformation is not entirely built on technology and platforms but on people.

As I mentioned at the outset, effective leaders recognize the importance of the three tenets: people, processes, and systems. The benefits of preserving, nurturing, and advocating for them in your organization will pay dividends.

Although the MDMP is more noticeable at the command level due to increased staffing requirements, the procedure still occurs across all command echelons, from senior general officer levels to the platoon leader conducting troop-leading operations.

Although the military also has an eight-step problem-solving process, it is more prescriptive than the MDMP, which is more descriptive and, therefore, more people-centric.

As you may observe, regardless of which version of the model is used, any excuses for avoiding deliberate planning are eliminated.

It forces leaders to become better time managers by triggering and assessing redundant plans and highlighting the need for them.

The MDMP is scaled down to accommodate the staffing requirements of smaller units and those at the tactical level, resulting in less rigid TLPs or Troop Leading Procedures.

Despite this, let us focus more on its parent, the MDMP, which, as you will find, encompasses the others, and its applicability in both the private and public sectors begins to unfold.

The process's results come to life through real-world events at the organization's lower levels. Additionally, it will become clear that planning this deliberately removes single points of failure and finger-pointing.

Chapter 2

"Treat your men like your beloved sons; they will follow you into the deepest valley."
Sun Tzu

Conditions Check

Scholarly literature theorizes that some leaders are born with innate skills. However, they are often born with leadership traits that are distinct and separate things.

Leadership skills are developed, taught, and honed over time. They are fostered and nurtured through repetition of successes and failures, mentorship, and critical thinking.

Building on previous thought, considering that one of the nine core Stoic beliefs is that we have all been given the inner resources we need to thrive, it is not surprising that Stoics such as Cleanthes and Panaetius held that human beings are endowed with these instincts toward virtue. We can succeed and live nobly if we learn to live consistently with our nature and duties.[7] Furthermore, our creativity is endless if we view ourselves as unfinished poems and life as the environment that provides the resources we need to write our best poetry.

In some ways, the Industrial Revolution and current-day technological developments are overwhelming examples of their thinking, codifying this point.

Interestingly, what has made this possible is people's will, drive, tenacity, and ability to take risks and look for the impossible. However, let's set aside the Stoics for a moment. Although their thinking was more old-fashioned, it is more applicable today in some respects.

But humor me, and let's take a more modern view. Evolutionary Psychology posits that the evolved human mind comprises a set of cognitive mechanisms, each specialized to learn, remember, and reason about distinct types of information.[8] We have long broken the mold of problem-solving supported by the rationale and research behind the theory of Evolutionary Psychology.

Evolutionary Psychology has played a crucial role in shaping who we are.[9] In some respects, our ethical and moral glide paths are built on the notion that our senses, power of choice, and ability to reason are already innately programmed. The MDMP uses this thinking and other concepts to extract the best from its leaders. These leaders, even when their ideas, if any, do not make the final cut, are imbued with the team concept over their desire to excel and succeed.

That is because the outcomes of these decisions benefit the team and, by extension, the individuals.

The MDMP exemplifies these various schools of thought in which people must collaborate to reach a single conclusion while eliminating single points of failure and finger-pointing.

At higher levels of military command, it is not surprising that leaders encourage the reading and study of historical battle-hardened general officers and their philosophies, tactics, and overall persona along with other leaders not just to broaden critical thinking skills but, more importantly, to get an advantage—an advantage over the competition and the enemy.

The same approach can be applied in both the public and private sectors to align with organizational objectives and personnel development. For the military, Sun Tzu is one such choice. Tzu was a renowned Chinese military general and strategist, best known for the work The Art of War, a discourse on military strategy.

Therefore, I thought it prudent to explore the importance of people, not through a military construct but from a more practical point of view, where his philosophies apply to leadership and management for the rest of the chapter.

Suppose you had told me that, as an eighteen-year-old getting ready to graduate high school, I would be a soldier, not just in any Army, but in the United States Army! Not only would I have laughed you out of the room, but I would also have looked at you with crazed bewilderment because the first was never a boyhood dream of mine.

The second would not have seemed rational at that moment. Mind you, there was no precedent for that thinking. Our family had never discussed immigrating to the United States, much less joining the army. Like my other classmates, I was just a kid with dreams of attending the University of the West Indies in Jamaica after high school.

But this book is not a memoir. It is about how my professional successes, both as a soldier and as a military consultant, have been built on friendships, partnerships, and relationships with people.

And how, if a semblance of the principles of military leadership is applied, how life-changing individuals and teams can be because of it.

Making people a priority sounds right, but it can also perpetuate the status quo of saying one thing and doing another, or virtue signaling. Observing something broken is merely an observation unless it is acted upon.

The assumptions underlying the observation above are often correct, and the frightening results and relevance of this phenomenon will become clearer later.

—

In groups, there is a predominance of one or, in some cases, multiple sub-groups sharing the same spaces, thus resulting in group dynamics.

The US Army's Basic and Advanced Individual Training (AIT) courses are tailored primarily for enlisting soldiers into the Army and present dynamic team challenges.

It did for me; I know it did for some of my teammates. For me, though, they were nothing earth-shattering or life-altering. Culture, testosterone, hubris, ego, and youth were all present. Given these variables, you would expect to encounter team challenges. However, they were in controlled environments.

That is, like the cadence lyrics say, "Everywhere I go, there's a Drill Sergeant there," watching your every move. If other dynamic team issues were at

play, they were done in close quarters and pri-
vately.

That is, either in the individual's mind or shared with like-thinking individuals behind closed doors.

Anything else was hashed out in supervised, competitive training events, to which we looked forward, such as the Puggle stick pit.

—

In contrast, one of my firsthand experiences with group dynamics in an uncontrolled environment (uncontrolled in this context refers only to distinguish it from the training environment, where daily freedoms to come and go are allowed in regular units) occurred in 2003.

My platoon, the civilian equivalent of a department in a medium-sized company, was attached as an added platoon to this new outfit and detached from our parent unit.

My first observations were that my soldiers were being mistreated, given the bulk of the physical work in preparation for combat.

I felt like we were the proverbial Redheaded Stepchildren. So, I wanted to approach the Commander quickly.

My platoon leader and immediate supervisor, Second Lieutenant Bright, a good man, had tried to warn me. He suggested I take the time to calm down before making my right, wrong. I was undeterred.

My approach was not conducive to good order and discipline, and later, I paid the price for my insubordinate approach. However, the corrective action was proper and focused on the problem, which is why I approached him in the first place. The absence of escalation was also immediately noticeable.

I had opened the door, a gesture some seniors often take to flex the power derived from their rank and position. It is universally acknowledged that organizations require effective leaders who must make tough, on-the-spot decisions to succeed.

Those who do will reap the results of motivated, empowered, and contributing teammates. In other words, leaders who do not use their power positively and misemploy it will act overbearingly.

On the more extreme ends and in a society more socially conscious than a decade ago, such leadership or lack thereof can even be considered abusive or bullying.

Captain Trump knew the door was open, but he never entered. He addressed the problem, not the individual.

Often, leaders exploit their ability to personalize issues, making it easy to denigrate and belittle subordinates, frequently disguised as corrective action.

This personal insight culminated in a lengthy conversation that eventually included my Platoon Leader, the other Platoon Sergeants, and the company's First Sergeant.

The latter of whom was more than a mentor to me. First Sergeant Level was a true soldier leader.

His soldiers loved and respected him. He was fair, frank, and reasonable. From then on, we became the gold standard for a Combat Service Support Company. Some of its convoy procedures were standardized throughout the theatre for other companies and outfits.

This is partly because some tactics, techniques, and procedures (TTPs) for convoy operations on

Middle Eastern streets, specifically city centers, had not yet been fully developed. As the enemy situation around us evolved, we learned and adapted to various methods on the job.

We captured and shared successes and shortcomings among each patrol leader in the company, as well as with others, during debriefs after each patrol.

What was significant about the encounter, and why I'm highlighting it here, is that it was part of that unit's team development. Where egos, arrogance, individual personalities, cultural norms, and traits are fleshed out and put aside.

They were not forgotten or dismissed; they were not prioritized. This laid the foundation for everything else we did. We were at the stage where leaders, in this case, my Commander and managers, could begin developing their teams.

This is the stage of the TLP where the Commander exercised his supervisory role and refined our plan. The cohesive team begins to materialize and take shape within this step. This was not always the case, as the Troop Leading Procedure concept has only recently been applied outside the combat arms realm.[10]

We previously discussed transformation and change agents. This was, and still is, a mutation in real-time. The military is no different in meeting transformational goals and seizing opportunities to change when they present themselves. Iraq and Afghanistan proved this point.

They directly attributed their success to the more than ten years of war and the collaborative efforts across all cohorts and branches, while often working outside traditional doctrinal roles that were necessary for their achievements to be possible.[11] I am proud to report that the unit was a tremendous success that year in Iraq, not because we were not challenged. The enemy, personal challenges, and team dynamics presented challenges to us. Still, we overcame it because of our willingness and ability to work, live, and survive collaboratively through problem-solving and military decision-making.

Captain Trump and his leadership team became remarkably successful leaders. I often check in on social media. Maintaining professional bonds is essential, even if those friendships and relationships have no direct ties to one's professional industry in the private and public sectors.

There is nothing wrong with asking for advice or help in dealing with a situation you may struggle with. Ergo, having and maintaining this professional network of friends and colleagues remains valuable to posts and continued careers.

Even more relevant are the impressions left on younger members of these groups, who have the potential to grow through repetitive behavior or paying it forward. The concept of iron sharpening iron is replicated throughout these exchanges. Sometimes purposefully done through formal exchanges or repeated everyday actions and behaviors that peers and subordinates emulate.

Chapter 3

"The heights by great men reached and kept…were not attained by sudden flight, but they, while their companions slept, were toiling upward in the night."

From The Ladder of St. Augustine by Henry Wadsworth Longfellow

Getting it Right

I have spoken with civilians and uniformed personnel about various subjects, ranging from mundane matters to more serious topics and trends in life and the military.

At least for me and to everyone's chagrin, the topics always find their way back to people, processes, and systems. It was during a rare break from a training exercise that I had my first real conversation about the impact of people on this paradigm in an informal setting.

Colonel Sep, who works in Special Forces and Special Operations, and my boss, walked into our workspace for a cup of coffee. For some clarity, Sep had only recently taken command of a conventional Army unit. Remember, his background and skill sets are unconventional.

I asked how things were going, and as I took a seat, several lessons emerged. We spoke for over thirty minutes, which is rare because he had not done that before. Possibly, it was because of time or because he was comfortable enough with me as a teammate to share.

Ultimately, Sep's concern was not how he would command—he knew that—but how he would relate to people. Again, keep in mind that he was the boss. Often, bosses are not concerned about how they will be perceived; the opposite is usually true. He wondered if he had the right people in the right places to offer him sound counsel. Another struggle was finding time for mentorship and development, as the operational tempo in the unit was brutal. Now, I know I mentioned that you would not encounter novel concepts. Well, the last runs rampant in organizations—the inability or lack of interest in mentorship. As Commander, he recognized that the problems he would face in a conventional setting depended on the unit's ability to make effective decisions.

Interestingly, it was a valid concern because our roles included being observers, coaches, trainers, and mentors to other units undergoing rotational training. Their success during those rotations hinged on using the MDMP to solve complex, sometimes multiple military dilemmas that we incorporated into their training plan.

It meant we could not be slackers in understanding the process and its applicability.

It would not be news to you if I told you that owning it is hard. Even harder is honest self-reflection. I suspect that what Sep was realizing was that, underneath all his street cred and operational achievements, with the tabs to prove it, he was an emotionally intelligent leader.

Those principles of emotional intelligence, acting by reflex, were triggered.

What he was realizing was that when we act decisively and quickly during a crisis and break away from our insular ways of thinking — and accept others' cultures and ideas — we realize how valuable they are. We can incorporate those traits into our toolkit.

His feelings of open-mindedness about how people would perceive him and his awareness of the importance of professional growth are the first of four indicators of emotionally intelligent leaders. You will also find that they make excellent listeners.

They understand that hearing is an involuntary reaction, while listening is an art. If you are already formulating a response, you cannot understand what is being said.

Teams operate more efficiently when communication is clear, understood, and free from ambiguity and personal desires that are entwined in the outcomes. They are not mind readers.

Emotionally intelligent leaders will not sugarcoat the truth. Sep, Trump, and others like them can navigate the passage between feelings and emotions.

A feeling is the result of an emotional reaction to something. EI leaders focus on the emotional responses from and external factors on the person. They avoid complicating others' feelings with how they handle emotions.

In part, as human beings, our feelings are biased because unconscious or conscious misconceptions influence them. Leaders do not have the time to weed through both nuances, so they deal with what triggered the feeling in the first place—the emotion or the catalyst. Finally, and this is a tough one, they apologize when they are wrong. This is a tough one because, for so long, and to some extent even today, people in charge, leaders, find it hard to admit they are wrong and apologize.

They perceive this process of self-reflection and correction as a weakness, whereas the opposite is true. It indicates inner strength and a willingness to admit error, especially if you are the decision-maker and are expected to be free from making errors.

I encourage you to set that notion aside because what is true is that as your subordinates emulate you, you are strengthening your organization's culture through your actions.

Sep struggled with this in some ways, but he succeeded in the two-plus years we worked together.

Another memorable experience involves another Special Forces Colonel, Mark. I also worked with Mark in a similar setting to Sep's.

Where Sep was concerned about how he would relate as Commander of a conventional brigade, Mark was worried about how he and his team of Special Forces observers would interact with traditional units when receiving feedback. Mark understood the complications involved in the different procedures and systems and, like Sep, wanted to get it right. When joint operations are conducted, communication gaps can arise from teams not always working together effectively. Time and space exacerbate this. Not all units are co-located, and the distance between teams can be hundreds of miles.

Whenever I was privy to discussions of who would be assigned where for the next training exercise, Mark's remedy was predicated on his liaison officer. Who would be his voice, and by extension, the operators' voices from strategic locations, providing sound counsel to a conventional Army general?

Sergeant Major G, Mark's Senior Enlisted Advisor, a gentle giant in so many ways, would say, *"Sir, anyone you trust that can answer the questions you ask at this table and similarly defend their suggestions as you would is the right choice."*

The point?

If they could answer Mark's questions and articulate their reasoning and rationale, considering his level of expertise, experience, and knowledge, then this would give Mark predictability.

But, as you may have noticed, all these decisions have one underlying theme: trust. Some say my observation is stating the obvious: *"Isn't that expected?"* I would say not always. Selecting someone to speak on your behalf is a critical decision.

Throughout my career, I have also seen several situations in which information and communication gaps were filled by people who were unarmed, unprepared, and out of their depth and selected as liaison officers. As a result, misaligned goals and duplicated efforts persisted, all of which were perpetuated by communication setbacks.

Chapter 4

> *"Who does not want to know that we notice and value them? And who might respond to us better when they feel that they matter? It cannot be overstated – it matters...that people matter."*
> Steve Goodier

Building Consensus

So far, the leaders we have discussed have been experts at their leadership challenges because they realized that leadership should not be a solitary endeavor. Leaders can draw on the skills and experiences of others and their own when making decisions, and they should.

Group thinking is problematic when there is a lack of diversity of thought or ideas. So, who these advisers and change agents are and how much trust the leader places in them are critical to the quality of that leader's judgment.

Again, this is a prominent point on the surface.

Look deeper at corporations and companies; you will see a culture of *this, which is who and what we have or were given, and we are making the best of it and* negatively projecting the self-disparaging notion that *our performance is solely aligned with whom we have* and sending implications that who you have may not be good enough.

Sep would make it a point to tell the junior officers during feedback sessions, *"There are two things you will not get more of in the drop-down menu of military operations: more time and more people."*

His point was not that the status quo is correct in that one must use what one has been *dealt with* as a negative and depressing situation, but as an opportunity. Take ownership of the challenge and make it work.

Don't stop or turn around at the first obstacle. Militarily speaking, leaders rarely have that choice. Instead, find ways to negotiate them or remove them. This removal and negotiation can be achieved with internal administrative processes in the public and private sectors. The military employs various methods and thresholds, depending on orders from echelons with the necessary approval authority. Ultimately, if the obstacle persists and meets one or more of the thresholds for military action, then it is addressed with force.

The bottom line is, do not let removable obstacles hinder your will. Imagine it this way: if you accept them in their youth, with their arrogance, inexperience, shyness, self-doubt, and all the other variables that come with immaturity and adolescence, then an opportunity is the inverse.

Based on those variables we just mentioned, people at this stage in their lives are more receptive and eager, or perhaps seeking something else—something different— for those who are not necessarily young but have been settling elsewhere for too

long. You have the challenge and opportunity to
mentor, shape, and participate in their maturation,
at least for a couple of years, and in most respects,
longer, in the private and public sectors.

You accomplish this while still having to get the
job done. That is challenging indeed, but the pay-
offs will be exponential. They are exponential because of reciprocal behavior, where teammates
share what they have learned by *paying it forward in
hopes of replicating the behaviors.*

This reciprocity can occur in any organization.

Unsurprisingly, researchers like social psychologist Edwin Hollander espouse that a leader's influence is interpersonal and depends on followers rec-
ognizing the leader's unique attributes.[12] But how
do they do this?

In a word?

Trust.

Leaders must develop trust across all echelons,
both within and outside their organization. Expect-
antly, there are barriers to this thinking. These junior leaders vary in age, demographics, and level of
life experience, which ties back to and reinforces
Sep's consideration.

Evidence shows that success is augmented
throughout the organization when followers are
treated as valued members, and management is
prepared to invest in improved performance.[13]

Building the organization's change initiatives and
missions to cultivate the existing culture is equally
valid. Consider Rudy Giuliani's actions immediately after and during the September 11, 2001, attacks. But this time, not from the construct of the individual leader, but the team he built around him

and their effects on the outcomes, not Giuliani's alone. In hindsight, the city and state of New York were the better for it.

Also, leaders in Boston, Massachusetts, should be given some notoriety for their actions after the Boston Marathon Bombing incident. The coalescing of separate emergency response teams towards one goal was textbook, given that they, like other large metropolises in the concept of time, had little of it to prepare for large-scale terrorist attacks post those of September 11, 2001. If you look more closely, you will find that not any one leader's actions drove the results, but rather the actions of the combined teams.

On the other hand, some notable failures come to mind. Enron, for example. In 2001, the company's executives knowingly falsely inflated the value of the company's stock, leading to one of the largest accounting scandals and bankruptcies in recent history.[14]

After an extensive investigation, it was revealed that egos and hubris primarily caused the problems. In this case, intentionally orchestrated single points of failure were built around individuals with nefarious intent.

Kenneth Lay, the disgraced CEO, was later arrested for his role in a wide-ranging scheme to defraud Enron by falsifying publicly reported financial results and making false and misleading public representations about Enron's business performance and financial condition.[15]

But the story here was the larger pool of those affected. Other than investors, the company's people—some of whom had given years and their reputations—were left holding the bag.

Another American landmark case that comes to mind is Boeing. Specifically, in 2019, it did not contain the fallout of two fatal crashes of one of its more actively used planes.[16] Missteps by management across the enterprise were often a nightly news occurrence, but more so at the top, despite red flag signals from its employees indicating wide-ranging issues.

In short, this behavior and poor decision-making led to Boeing's stock price plummeting, which affected investors, some of whom had long-held retirement accounts heavily invested in the company's stock.

Investors from both individual and institutional spectrums who understood market moves and economics and invested based on those principles, rather than poor leadership, were all affected.

More importantly, a culture built around its people, safety record, and beacon of American ingenuity was damaged and questioned.

This fact underscores the importance of a value-added culture within an organization.

A strategy at odds with a company's culture is doomed.

This thinking codifies Sep's and my earlier point that it is not always about the culture or acquiring new and shiny objects, but instead being aware of where to make changes. And what, if anything, can be changed?

Colonel Retired Shot is an avid believer, author, supporter, and, in some respects, historian of the MDMP.

I mention Shot here because one of his favorite parts of the process, he once told me (from the private back briefs that occur between Commanders and their subordinate Commanders), and to the earlier point on age, was, *"When that young man walked away after his confirmation brief to me…At that moment, I knew he had it; it was not only a confirmation of his understanding of the mission but also a testament to his ability to grasp it. But that moment in which, for him, the light comes on. The moment when he has put meaning to his purpose."*

For Shot, those are memorable moments, not just for *the light coming on*. In Shot's experience, these were the early years after the Vietnam Conflict, in which young soldiers were not inclined to follow good order and discipline; moreover, getting it right.

As I mentioned earlier regarding Enron, the first observation is not always an accurate reflection of the culture. Things may not need changing.

Culture is not something that can be easily manipulated.

Attempts to grab it and twist it into a new shape never work because you can't grab it.[18] Attitudes within the culture may need to be changed. Leaders can achieve this through evaluations and counseling. That is because culture changes only after you successfully alter people's actions, and the new behavior produces some group benefits for a period. After seeing the connection between the latest actions and performance improvement,[19]

To achieve these, leaders must incorporate nebulous aspirations and goals early in the developmental plan and revisit them at a time that best suits the organization and its teammates.

What you cannot do is neglect to say and define them early in the hiring and teambuilding process. In the military, commanders often spend thirty days in *a left-seat, right-seat arrangement* alongside their counterparts to assess the unit's capabilities while conducting other required tasks before assuming command.

Incoming commanders get to peek *behind the curtain* before officially taking the helm. This gives them a head start in visualizing and describing their intentions to their incoming team.

Yet, there is another way to look at it. Approaching it as a continuation of success by getting their peers' *feedback on the center of gravity* is not cheating.

Input on what drove their successes and what challenges existed in other areas helps the incoming commander establish conditions to alleviate knowledge-sharing gaps and stovepiping. Interestingly, this interplay inadvertently creates another helpful procedure that permeates the organization down to the lowest levels.

Let us refer to it as the continuity process.

—

A system leaders use to store lessons learned, templates, case studies, techniques, and procedures that have been successful in the past. This process can be digitized, analogized, combined, and managed by a dedicated individual, which the military refers to as a knowledge manager.

When time does not allow for a window into the organization beforehand, tailor your aims and non-vague goals to the existing cultural traits embodying good order and discipline. Then, match and support the current strategy.

Overly anxious leaders want to make changes to make an initial impact. I caution against this because it sends the wrong message. The crux of this book is the impact of people on change initiatives, which are grounded in procedures and systems. In that vein, take the time to assess before implementing change.

You may ask, what is lost if you do not? Consider these: trust, integrity, and unity of effort.

It is harder to win any of them back. You will also quickly discover that you waste considerable time and resources trying to regain them.

Even if you do, there is the question of integrity and believability among your people. How much effort will teammates give to you if they perceive your changes as unnecessary?

Furthermore, what will their perceptions be if those changes are aligned with questionable integrity? Change is dynamic and emotional for some, so tread lightly when addressing it. All issues are leadership issues, but not every issue is a must-fix-now issue.

The intent is to build collaborative teams that, as they work together, reinforce existing traits and develop new ones through the formal and informal processes and systems that structure their work.

The catalyst for change is often, if not due to, a shift in people's needs and desires.

The military is not immune to these changes, and I would suggest, in keeping with our problem-solving theme, that it be prudent and deliberate in its approach, as you may recall.

The list is long, including the years of the *Don't Ask, Don't Tell policy* under then-President Clinton and the subsequent change to that policy. Other issues include accommodations for women serving in combat arms units, religious practices, hairstyle standards, physical fitness evaluation tests, and the inclusion of women in Special Forces.

—

Before we dive deeper, I am compelled, if not remiss, to emphasize that compromise, tolerance, and acceptance are not weaknesses. On the contrary, they are the bedrock on which successes are built. Because at the heart of all these and other challenges were people. And, at the heart of all the solutions are people. Yet, if I have led you to believe people-centric issues are easy, I am sorry—the hazards of unintended assumptions.

The reality is that they are hard. Yet, the Stoics would tell you that you are innately armed with the necessary tools to get after it. More recent science on the growth of human initiative, intuition, and cognitive development would support their argument. If you choose, you could add the benefits of the MDMP to this paradigm.

As we continue our descent, below are concerns, comments, considerations, and discussions from two prominent decision-makers that I found prudent and vital during my research for the book.

In repealing *Don't Ask, Don't Tell*, President Obama said the following: *"For we are not a nation that says, 'don't ask, don't tell." We are a nation that says, "Out of many, we are one." We are a nation that welcomes the service of every patriot. We are a nation that believes that all people are created equal. Those are the ideals that generations have fought for. Those are the ideals that we uphold today."*

It was not so much the speech itself that was significant, but rather why. President Obama's statement was grounded in our nation's historical development and institutions that place people at the center.

In my own experiences, the military has prioritized people through formal and informal sensing sessions, reviews, and discussions in search of solutions. Platitudes are meaningless without action. Politicians are particularly adept at them.

Yet, despite your political leanings, I found the juxtaposition of a significant piece of *our* American history, a quoted line from the Jamaican motto, and a symbol from its coat of arms that reads, *'out of many, one people,'* and a bit of my personal history, all appropriate in this instance.

You may ask why.

Affected individuals must be part of their destinies. Jamaica's national heroes did that for its independence. Should all Americans and service members continue to be part of the long national tradition of upholding the values upon which the republic was founded?

I would offer that they were doing so. Lost on some was the reality that, during these policies, servicemembers were deployed worldwide, sometimes in unstable or hostile environments, silently doing the nation's bidding.

—

Although the nation did not know it actively, they were a part of the Decision-Making Process immediately and years after September 11, 2001. President George Bush was aware of it and took it personally.

He was adamant about a particular part of his speech for the nation's retaliation to Congress for September 11, 2001. His adamance regarded the length and stressed his team and writers to get it right.

He wanted the speech's length to convey to Americans the potentially protracted nature of the war effort. He did not want to create unrealistic expectations of results. Further, I suspect he lamented how much Americans were willing to sacrifice in the name of retaliation.

He, too, like within the MDMP, where the proverbial Doves and Hawks exist, had to temper expectations.

In the final draft, he said, *"Our response involves far more than instant retaliation and isolated strikes."* ~ *"Americans should not expect one battle but a lengthy*

—

In 2005, a civilian demonstration of the MDMP model in action took place. I associate it with MDMP under the three tenets we have discussed: people, processes, and systems.

Consider this: In Texas, as the saying goes, they do things big.

Returning from Iraq in 2005 through Dallas-Fort Worth was a fantastic experience. We were surprised to be greeted by Vietnam veterans who thanked *us for our service* while handing out baggies full of welcome-home gifts.

Along with them were seniors from the local community who had volunteered and worked with the airlines to prioritize all our flights heading to the West Coast from Dallas, ensuring minimal, if any, wait times for our next flight.

The irony of the situation was that the same was not true for those veterans when they returned from Vietnam. Instead, they were ridiculed, spat on, and treated with dislike and arrogance.

Yet, despite their myopia, their emotional intelligence and sense of brother and sisterhood were activated by what they perceived as being in the same fight. What are the alternative courses of action? If they had chosen to stay home with their families or alone, no one would have known, and I wouldn't have had a story to share and make a point.

The veterans could have supported us quietly and shown indifference to a public display.

Yet, they did not.

The volunteers were an extension of the larger family team, liaising with the local community, airline, and airport authority to allocate space, set up, and provide Thanksgiving meals for returning soldiers.

The experience was surreal, emotional, and memorable, all rolled into pure unexplained appreciation.

When you clear the suffocating issues, such as dislike and animosity, that we share as a society and sometimes use to become callous human beings, you see *the forest for the trees*—the impact of people serving others, especially when they do not have to or when there is no need. Things become clear.

It was reassuring to see the veterans, with whom we have a deep connection, still involved, sharing in our successes; as I said, it was and still is an impactful eye-opener. I have given it thought over the years and continue to do so. What thoughts were going through the Vietnam veterans' minds at the airport? I would imagine something similar to what was happening in mine. I was thinking—and still do—oh, how times change.

—

President Bush's administration ushered in an unprecedented era of interoperability across federal, private, and international agencies, despite some people's concerns about the constitutionality of specific approaches.

The successes from information sharing alone were justification for some, while other methods were, as I said, open to debate on their constitutionality.

There is an argument to be made regarding extending our retaliation for September 11, 2001 — emotions, poor and inaccurate advice, and a lack of communication predicated the conflict.

That resonated with some then and still does with some today regarding Iraq. For our purposes, interoperability may have been pure genius or the result of recommendations from military advisers because it read like a military document. Of course, my assumption is predicated on the interoperable Military Decision-Making Process.

We have proven it on several occasions, to our and the world's relief, with joint partners and have used it in planning and executing large-scale combat operations, such as Operation Desert Storm more recently, and historically with the French and British in World War II.

Interoperability is people-centric, and therefore, like other people-centric processes, it is challenging.

Despite that, we have executed the procedures seamlessly.

In 1989 and early 1990, the late Generals Norman Schwarzkopf and Colin Powell created a war plan not seen since World War II.

A strategy built and trusted to go well, based on tactical operations, but more on interoperability.

Interoperability refers to the set of systems, people, and processes that work together to achieve a common, agreed-upon goal.

As I said, not easy.

The results of the plan were immediate. Not only were the Iraqis quickly surrendering in droves because of weapon superiority coupled with the results of interoperability, but the apparent indifference to the junior leaders' input—that bottom-up refinement necessary to feed decision-making and problem-solving—was night and day.

And that is saying it nicely.

Where coalition leaders were tailoring their decisions to the feedback from various sensors, primarily the human sensor—the Iraqi leadership was busy on television with outlandish rhetoric and platitudes while their Army fell apart.

They ignored the feedback from their junior leaders on the front at their country's and people's peril.

Interestingly, General Schwarzkopf also said, when addressing leadership, *"You learn far more from negative leadership than positive leadership because you learn how not to do it." This lesson was lost on* many members of the Iraqi government and the Army.

Sadly, for the Iraqi people, they were the same: a single point of failure. We Americans must be cautious not to repeat the errors of past administrations and policies. Similarly, global leaders must think the same when participating in or negotiating outcomes involving people. In chapter one, we briefly discussed the errors corporations, businesses, and governments make when they ignore the tenets of people, processes, and systems, with people at the core.

We have discussed two landmark leadership failures so far. However, they were primarily individuals who failed.

The upcoming six errors, in aggregate, represent more systemic failures and continue to highlight the issues associated with neglecting the impacts of our policy intents on people—specifically, the neglect of their input and influence on outcomes.

—

Before we do, though, consider this: in the airline industry, in which any known and unseen variable, such as weather, technology, or strike, interrupts the entire enterprise and processes due to CEOs and C-Suite staff who, although intelligent people, fail to include these variables' effects when they forecast inadequately.

Although a convenient choice for travel, the airline industry, in part, is a single point of failure, one we have become highly dependent upon and one that is unlikely to change.

It has not changed because so many vested entities are unwilling due to economic, political, and social impacts. This insular thinking is why many unprofitable airlines remain in business despite years of reporting substantial losses to creditors, investors, and the traveling public's confidence in their service.

Closing a sizable, unprofitable airline would be unpalatable for all stakeholders, as it would involve the loss of thousands of jobs, inconvenience to hundreds of thousands of travelers, and millions of dollars in losses for the airline's creditors. Unsurprisingly, a significant portion of the profit margin is spent on customer incentives and loyalty perks, leaving actual profits unrealized.

Yet, not all for-profits are penalized for failure. But now, unlike the airline industry, where *it is what we have until a new light bulb comes along*, the following discussions have an acute sense of urgency.

They are urgent because, like the airline industry, lives are at stake.

Error 1

Our initial plans immediately following tactical operations in Iraq did not account for vacuums.

Or, more honestly, the wiser voices in the room regarding their creation and its impacts were either drummed out or explicitly suppressed.

However, voids, if not accounted for, create common problems that, unlike conventional warfare, are much harder to control and manage.

The results of which are disenfranchised people. Sadly, for years, both Iraq and Afghanistan were at that end. We all experienced too many losses as a result. We eventually got it right in Iraq.

Error 2

Disappointingly, the same report cannot be said of Afghanistan. It still has a vacuum. I say 'still' because the entity that filled the existing void left by our and others' untimely exits years earlier is still there. And not just there; they are in power. It is like another *'oops; we did it again' moment for the United States,* in which we uproot an ally in the making and leave without a policy.

Imagine you are a young Afghan girl getting ready for school, or an Afghan boy thinking you are done entertaining grown men in performing the *cultural dance* called *bacha,* which is nothing more than child prostitution and slavery.

And you hear about the sudden withdrawal of some 18,000 U.S. civilian contractors, which turns off the Afghan military's planes and helicopters, leaving ground troops without close air support and emergency coordination, including medical evacuation, and rendering the reputable special forces immobile and out of action?[20] Well? You do not have to.

It occurred and was on our watch! As if that was not bad enough, the still viable equipment we left behind in our haste went to terrorists, left behind to be used to terrorize their citizens.

Primarily women and children. These are known terrorists with whom the better part of the Western world has vowed not to negotiate.

If you think our enemies and allies are not paying attention, think again. We may have to send Americans to fight to fill these vacuums that were poorly handled. We may have to, again, win hearts and minds among young men ideologically twisted and highly bent on revenge. We may have to do this on nonlinear, conventional battlefields, a costly lesson in lives and wealth learned in Afghanistan and Iraq.

Error 3

The previous administration's inability to address pressing Middle Eastern political issues, its withdrawal from talks and policies that were at least stabilizing and tethered to meaningful dialogue, and its disinterest in listening have exacerbated the problems.

In his *Foreign Affairs* essay titled, *The Middle East Abhors a Vacuum*, Kenneth Pollack warns that *"the United States' withdrawal appears to be unleashing a predictable struggle among Middle Eastern states over which will take the United States' place at the region's head."*

On the surface, some will say this seems inevitable, even plausible. But the rest of what Pollack had to say should concern anyone paying attention. *"Some are willing to fight hard to win that crown, and others are willing to fight just as hard to prevent someone else—or anyone claiming it."*

To the uninformed, untrained eye, politicians and governments would have us think there is *nothing to see here; move along!* Stewing under the umbrella, disguised as *nothing to see,* lie active human volcanoes waiting to erupt.

We are often inundated with *big news* items on cable news networks—and if we are honest brokers, it is not news or newsworthy half the time.

Unless we tailor our news channels to what we genuinely want to be informed about, we will not be aware of the gaps that emerge worldwide.

Human volcanoes have been built under pressure and squeezed by the oppressive policies and actions of those in charge. Some are on the brink of erupting, and the question should not be if but when they will explode.

Vacuums in which people are being slaughtered at their neighbors' hands. Because leadership in those regions and, in some instances, with supported policies of the West, disenfranchises and places entire cultures into untenable diasporas and continuous civil conflicts by simple exploitation.

These lacunas are created because people are often inadvertently or intentionally left out of the equation.

Chapter 5

"If you always do what you've always done, you'll always get what you've always got."
Henry Ford

Ignore them at your Peril

Error 4

Having plausible deniability due to diplomatic cover is not an excuse for what occurs when vacuums are filled by marginalized, amorphous, and sometimes belligerent groups that are excluded from problem-solving and decision-making.

And when war has become a bargaining tool, a way of life, and even a mode of governance,[21] the problems increase exponentially.

In Africa, these problems of vacuums play out daily, monthly, and yearly on the continent.

Government and military Commanders in Africa are complicit in the hostility that occurs because they, like large industrial and military complexes throughout the West and Europe, realize that wars can be profitable. Jason Kearns,[22,] also writing for *Foreign Affairs*, in his essay, *Rebels Without a*

Cause gives this example, *"Unlike groups before them that aimed to overthrow governments or secede, these new groups seek to extract resources from the state and residents, involve themselves in local governance, and offer young men rebellion is usually extremely masculine-a means of survival and dignity."*

Mind you, these are not leaders selected through any democratic operation. Still, they instill their will through fear and terror.

Ask yourselves, what makes them do this? The following two errors should illuminate the current thinking.

Error 5

Leaders who exploit those they represent are single points of failure. It is even more frightening when, in some cases, insurgents have developed symbiotic relationships with the governments they nominally oppose.[23]

Gone are the days when political and social rioting, pressure on governments through strikes, and student presence in the streets were enough to turn the tide. Today, violence is the method of choice, especially in Africa. There seems to be no multi-faceted angle or means of communication needed in violence, except for the perpetrators.

I say that because there have been no changes to the status quo in past wars and years.

According to Kearns, another underlying factor in the violence is that *"most of Africa's insurgencies are repeat civil wars."* Every civil conflict on the continent is playing out on top of the ruins of, and, more importantly, on top of, social networks, worldviews, and grievances associated with previous episodes of violence.[24] Why can concepts embedded in the MDMP not be applied here? Instead, the same principles in the rooms make the same decisions based only on what they deem necessary.

Why can't fresh faces and ideas from among the disenfranchised be in the room? I concede that the problem sets to which the MDMP methodologies apply typically differ from those on the African continent. However, I do not aim to undermine or diminish the magnitude of the issues. I would even concede that the format of the United Nations, NATO, and other governmental and non-governmental organizations is structured this way.

With that in mind, it begs the question, why can't they ever find a solution? The process of involving people and canceling groupthink, in which those in the *ingroup* (who are often present in the room) and those who stand to benefit are excused, would open doors to compromise.

Any change initiative will benefit from collaboration and consensus-building around several central, similar themes, decisions, ideas, and potential solutions. We cannot continue to have peace deals that marginalize groups, no matter who they are.

For example, the peace deal in 2003 in Congo marginalized one of the most potent belligerents, the Congolese Rally for Democracy, a faction that returned to war [25] years later. The examples we have discussed are evidence of a broken reciprocal process marred by single points of failure. The lack of alternatives during the deal-making process further exacerbates the issues.

Error 6

Keeping the discussion in Africa because the examples are so prevalent, let us discuss destabilization. Destabilizing fighters in the context of reformation. Feeble attempts at reforming fighters, if any, were made after the Army offered few alternative livelihoods for former combatants.

They sidelined formerly powerful commanders, breeding resentment and spawning many new armed groups led by army defectors. [26]

This phenomenon was briefly in play in the early months and years following the Iraq War. Those who persisted in violence against America and its interests were removed.

Others were brought to the bargaining/dividing table. Thus, the results indicate that the MDMP model can and is used in diplomacy and politics. The United States military chaired many of the abovementioned meetings.

The players must also have meaningful, unbiased, and vested interests in the outcomes for the specific country, not for factions or segments.

They must be vetted and have no questionable ties to financial or other entities they influence.

However, before we can discuss change, explain how decision-makers should conduct their processes, and even offer the MDMP as a model, we must first understand how and why nations use conflict and people as a bargaining tool for fatally flawed problem-solving, without realizing that this approach is doomed from the outset.

They are doomed because they are predicated on personal opportunities of greed and personal gain—the conflict war version of Enron. Why does this perverse symbiosis exist between governments and rebel groups that oppose them?

The answer lies in another conflict in our recent past. Dr. Jacqueline Whitt,[27] a United States Army War College lecturer, asks the following profound question:

"Is the cautionary tale for strategists about the dangers of imperial overstretch and prolonged
wars or the tragedy of abandoning an ally in its time of greatest need?"

It gives us even more to contemplate, especially in light of the Afghanistan withdrawal fiasco—more questions to ask our leaders.

More questions to ask ourselves. Questions such as, *"Do we have the appetite for another war?" "Are we comfortable seeing the coffins come home draped in the flag on the nightly news?"*

To caveat Dr. Whitt's question, *"Are we comfortable abandoning those we promised we would support, knowing the potential long-term costs?"*

These are tough questions, I yield. Pardon if I am understating their complexities and do not purport to know the answers except to overstate the obvious from a soldier's perspective—a perspective based on my earlier assertions of having to win hearts and minds again.

Where vacuums are created, we run the risk of also developing enemies. And to Whitt and Kearns's point, in some instances, repeat enemies. Dr. Whitt adds that the *lessons* of Vietnam depend on perspective and interpretation.

I agree with her and encourage governments, non-profits, politicians, readers, and business executives to heed her observation, keeping in mind that a person's perception is their reality until it changes.

Best Practices to Section I

Own clearly stated problems early and address the enterprise and the media with the truth as it becomes known. Leaders face conflict and problems head-on, encouraging and building cohesive teams around them to counsel.

The military thrives on this concept, and it is fundamental. It does not point fingers or blame. They own it and build consensus around a standard picture.

They seek the center of gravity and friction points and operate from them. As mentioned earlier, these principles are not new or novel ideas. The military has just demonstrated that they do it better.

The military is good at embracing the power of people and challenging its leaders' perceptions of that concept. It checks egos and suppresses the *"I" mindset* in team events and training. It is in the culture to break habits that are toxic to growth and problem-solving.

Practices like *"We have always done it this way" and "We recognize problems, but what will change?" "Nothing ever does!" Providing* military examples of these

leaders would be a chapter in itself. It would be dis-
ingenuous of me not to state openly that the Military Decision-Making Process is not a panacea.

Admittedly, some macroeconomic problems require
much more tailored and coordinated approaches.
Still, the procedures' micro benefits benefit organizations of any size. However, they must be structured around the right people, strategies, and systems with the resources to find solutions to complex
problems.

Its iterative nature allows for collaboration and personal and team growth. It cannot be tailored to all
civilian scenarios. Still, we spoke briefly, and I will
expand on the importance of liaisons here.

Liaison Officers facilitate communication between
elements of an organization to ensure mutual understanding and unity of purpose and action. In the
military, liaison is the most employed technique for
establishing and maintaining close, continuous,
physical communication between commands.[28]

Where communication gaps exist in the military,
they are filled with a liaison officer or non-commissioned officers.

Doing so is often where digital communication is
hindered by time and space, and is not readily
available, in addition to requiring a physical presence. Hence, the officer bridges that gap—similarly,
sending elected or selected people on another's be-

half is also essential. Liaising is the act of individuals working for and providing their best advice and
counsel on behalf of their superiors, often in a political or military context.

Community representatives chosen by the local
populace, albeit a nonstandard democratic procedure (if we use Africa as a template), can do the
same. *What would that look like?*

Begin by speaking in that person's language. And
by that, I do not mean linguistically. Align the
change agents through commonality instead. Begin
with a culture where individuals can relate to an
analogous situation because they have relevant experience—people like scholars, academics, and representatives who are not politicians.

Why must they be politicians at all? The MDMP
methodology encourages team members to proac-
tively seek information about their functional areas.
Functional areas in this context refer to the expertise
of these individuals, which drives robust discussions around similar themes.

Where conflicting ideas are fleshed out, opinions
are tailored to the problem, and no other external,
often personal agenda topics cloud and overshadow
the reasons for being in these rooms.

The key is utilizing their empirical evidence, experience, and expertise to develop courses of action
through informed decision-making. They could
drive more meaningful discussions while avoiding

focus groups orchestrated by politicians with charts.

Where are the trustworthy change agents who grew up in poverty and the slums? Those tired of the proverbial *kicking of the can down the road*? Too often, politicians and governments appease people with their ingrained values and beliefs, which are usually embedded in their policy proposals. That is the absolute worst first step. Necessity, not ideology, should dictate policy.

The needs of the many should be the foundation from which a meaningful approach arises.

Consider this: the MDMP objective regarding an attack mission is not to push one enemy soldier off a military objective but rather to dislodge the entire battalion, including its equipment.
All available resources are tasked and prioritized towards that end. Suppose your goal is to eradicate poverty and promote economic development and prosperity. In that case, the policy should be based on the principles associated with the needs of that goal. Moreover, all available resources, like the attack mission, must be allocated towards that end.

Equally, the stupidity of attempting to speak the language of a culture to win votes or push forward some policy is just as appalling. Any handler coaching a politician or anyone else to do that should be fired.

Not to mention all those who try to do it horribly. In their pandering, they mistakenly compare their cultural norms to everyday issues their constituents experience, which is often contextually offensive and degrading.

Do not push your religion, values, and norms as the first or only premise from which you will negotiate. They do not need your faith. They often do not need your economic or political theories. What they need is recognition and inclusivity in access to resources. Yes, not everyone will know how to access and exploit the benefits of these resources, but the downstream availability of jobs in companies and corporations that do will help ease poverty levels in those regions hardest hit by ineffective economic and political policies—leading to recognition in capital and governance.

These are not handouts, mind you, as some cynics would have you think. These are measurable compromises that benefit everyone. They are equitable.

Using Africa, which is rich in natural resources, as an example, why can't a model like that of the Alaska dividend payment apply? That is where citizens participate in the revenue from these natural resources. Imagine a different outcome from the current ones if only we were genuinely willing. We are far too eager to implement changes that are *us*-based and not *them*-based. We have not tried solutions like these before, and I know change can be painful. We are impatient even when we do. We often set unachievable or unrealistic timelines for the things we implement, seeking immediate results. Some argue that this is an overly simplistic approach. I would counter, *"Why must your procedure be complicated?"*

A step-by-step, tiered, gradual approach that amplifies the elements that work and eliminates or restructures those that do not produce desired results is better than a cumbersome, often misunderstood, and motivation-sapping system.

Still, the established leadership must have an appetite for these inputs and be willing to make compromises. They cannot and should not be dismissed. The current results are indicative of this continued failure.

A Liaison Officer's primary skill set is that they are well-read and versed in the subject matter to which they are assigned.

Being assertive, personable, approachable, and willing to compromise, when given the opportunity, are all valuable assets.

I know that some problems have both visible and invisible complexities, which may require more advanced skill sets. Still, the ones mentioned here will suffice as a starting point. Placing people in the same environment to work on issues closely tied to their lives, for which their decisions have a direct impact, is a more plausible scenario that can yield results that cannot be overstated.

Mutual interests, a common goal, and fairness will facilitate more meaningful, robust discussions that lead to the best possible outcome.

People are the driving force behind any change initiative or exercise in that context. They are the bedrock and foundation of the MDMP. Getting results requires planning, problem-solving, deliberate, tedious, and people-centric attitudes.

Results where there is only one outcome, an outcome that benefits the majority, not just the few adept at exploitation. The MDMP has no agenda other than getting results.

Before we move on, a cautionary note: if you do not involve people in the solution with the proper problem-solving attitude, you will find that they quickly become a significant part of your problem.

Chapter 6

"If you define the problem correctly, you almost have the solution."
Steve Jobs

Synergy

Military procedures can be measured for operational effectiveness as the various phases of an operation unfold. Soldiers within the MDMP operate similarly to vehicle gages. They continuously monitor, assess, analyze, and make recommendations. The military refers to this as the operations process. In the military, as in broader industries, datasets can and are used to achieve goals.

However, these are specific and explicitly aligned with situations where human feedback is unavailable. That makes the operations process people-centric, like the others we have discussed.

The Army's framework for exercising mission command is decentralized execution, tailored around different mission requirements and orders from higher headquarters.

The concept leverages the human element, emphasizing trust, willpower, initiative, judgment, and creativity. This creativity is crucial and is reflected during operations.

It drives the planning, preparation, execution, and continual process assessment.[29] All those tenets, as well as those of the MDMP, are deliberate. This is not accidental.

At the heart of the concept is the central idea that commanders, supported by their team, are crucial — *(Crucial because this is where the alleviation of single points of failure gets its genesis. Imagine a hub-spoke concept in which the higher command is the hub, and the subordinate commands and Commanders are the spokes*—drive the conceptual and detailed planning necessary to understand, visualize, and describe their operational environment.

It enables them to articulate and socialize their decisions, direct, lead, and continuously assess operations.[30] Several principles guide this central idea. Four, to be exact.

The leader drives the process by making decisions using critical and creative thinking. They also build and maintain situational understanding.

Let's focus on the last two because they are more people-centric than the preceding two.

More importantly, they encourage collaboration and dialogue.[31]

Knowing that, is it fair to say people are the nucleus of this central idea? And that the information they provide is even more critical to this thinking and mindset. But what if the information they provide is flawed? And is the culture of the organization, or organizations when speaking jointly, infested with individual participants who stovepipe information?

Is it fair to say that the system is flawed, with single points of failure?

—

Frustrated during operations involving the hunt for known and suspected terrorists, Kyle Lamb, Special Operations soldier and author, wrote in his book *Leadership in the Shadows,*

"As an organization, the U.S. military is particularly good at its job, but has limitations. Some of these limitations are real, and some are very real. In other words, some restrictions impact the military's effectiveness in accomplishing its mission." His assessment is accurate so far, but that wasn't all.

*"So, after a couple of years of the system not working satisfactorily, we had to wake up! We had to get **everyone** at the table to contribute to hunting these men to the ends of the earth together."*

When cooperation in communication is lost, and collaboration and communication are inhibited, the result is a loss in productivity or momentum, as in Lamb's case. Lamb's Dilemma is a case study that demonstrates the importance of not having insular processes, such as leadership approaches. The entire enterprise must be able to understand them seamlessly. It should not be cumbersome and overly time-consuming. Insularity is one thing for specific groups and skill sets. Yet, when a shared understanding of the proposed objective or mission is ambiguous, and not all teams share the same information, inherently duplicate efforts permeate the organization.

As such, missions are more complicated to accomplish. Momentum is lost. Resources are strained, and people are burned out because they have been duplicating efforts for so long.

Another factor affecting collaboration is stove piping or hoarding of information, which is a showstopper in any team hypothesis.

Some view the phrase *knowledge is power* as a blueprint for personal advancement through hoarding information. Each new piece of data they gather is jealously guarded and used for their agenda.[33]

You may have heard an adage: *You will never see a U-Haul behind a Hearse.* The thinking behind the saying is that you cannot take it with you to your final act. So why stovepipe and keep what you know close hold instead of sharing to grow stronger teams and organizations? Lamb did not imply or say it.

Still, I suspect his frustrations rested on the coordination and collaboration needed among other shadow and named agency operators in the hunt for terrorists. In their final report to the President and Congress, the 9/11 Commission[34] avouched his frustrations, writing,

"We recommend establishing a National Counterterrorism Center, built on the foundation of the existing Terrorist Threat Integration Center. Breaking the older mold of national government organizations, this NCTC should be a center for joint operational planning and intelligence staffed by personnel from various agencies."

What you should know and what is interesting is that, by their admission, they cited the development of this joint center in part *"in the same spirit that guided the military's creation of unified joint commands!"* We already know that interoperability is a concept built on the premise that teams must collaborate and communicate to solve complex problems.

As mentioned earlier in Chapter Four, these joint commands had precedence and street cred built on their previous successes, so it should come as no surprise that the commission honored that.

Suppose the Military Decision-Making Process is the key ingredient in a potent drug's efficacy. Then, interoperability is the petri dish in which the experiment occurs.

The opposite of interoperability is disconnection or incompatibility, where elements do not complement each other well.

Imagine this scenario: Liz, the general manager of a high-end luxury brand, departs after successfully initiating and implementing a culture of productivity.

A culture with productivity returns doubling in previous years, with substantial returns on shareholder investments, and remedying a reputation tarnished by the last management and processes.

Now, imagine Liz taking all the methods and systems she had built and not sharing them with the rest of the culture. What do you think will become of the culture without shared values? Is she stove piping operational information?

Do you still feel the investment returns on the top and bottom lines will continue? And where knowledge management is non-existent, are their processes and systems lost?

Let us agree that culture is people-centric—the shared attitudes, values, goals, and practices that characterize an institution or organization.[35]

Then, we must ask problematic questions, such as how well-meaning leaders and managers can allow such behaviors and techniques to occur under their watch. Lamb and his team asked related questions about themselves and the processes, and they remedied their situation of communication and sharing. Lamb said,

"To improve this process, we needed everyone at the table to tell everyone else what they knew and needed to get done. To be more successful, the man on the ground needed to speak directly with the intelligence officer, who knew the personality they were tracking. We needed everyone to be aware of what everyone else was thinking and doing. We needed knowledge dominance."

Achieving that dominance would only be through collaboration, and they did. As a result of this continued collaboration, the current state of play on *the scoreboard for deterring terrorist acts is that the good guys are winning, and the bad guys are not.*

Winning doesn't mean being complacent and letting our guard down, either. It means remaining ever vigilant and prepared. It is not only military leadership that must contend with these questions but also find meaningful ways to address them and return to people-centric problem-solving. Remember in Chapter One when retired General Dubik said, *"Tactically, trust and confidence result from how confident soldiers are in themselves, their leaders, and the systems designed to increase the probability of their survival and success?"*

Well, if your systems negate the intangibles to which Dubik alludes, where constant reassessment and refinement, from top-down to bottom-up, are absent, then, to Lamb's point, if synchronization is lost, operations are doomed.

This is not only true in the military operational context but also in other contexts. It also applies to small-business conference rooms, corporation boardrooms, C-suites, and family dinner tables. This constant reassessment and refinement don't come from wishful thinking.

The adage *"practice makes perfect"* isn't just an adage. I have found that it is much more than that. It can be a poignant reminder of the contrary and profoundly true.

Not only does a battle buddy trust that his teammate will be there should he need him to cover fire during a movement or provide security, but he also has the trust and confidence that he knows *how* to use the rifle.

Training is the only way to achieve this level of trust and confidence. Leaders cannot abdicate their responsibility in this role.

One of the Commanders' primary responsibilities in the military is planning and resource training.

Extensive sports franchises spend millions to acquire top talent. Still, the ones that win championships repeatedly have cornered what it is to build teams that train hard and win together.

You owe it to the stakeholders and team.

Chapter 7

"Anyone who has never made a mistake has never tried anything new."
Albert Einstein

The One–Third–Two–Third Rule

The theories of trust and confidence will play out as expected, depending on several other variables. One of those variables is time. Like platitudes, saying the previous is easy. But unless acted upon, the observation is useless. What am I getting after? Only someone living under a rock would disagree that trust and confidence in a team are dynamic traits and that allocating and being willing to invest time in their development is sensible and pragmatic.

But how do we get there, and are Commanders and managers willing to allocate time for the training to build synchronization, confidence in each other, the equipment, and trust? Commanders focus most of their energies on effective planning during military decision-making.

Time is a critical variable in operations. Therefore, time management is essential in planning. Whether done deliberately or rapidly, all planning

requires the skillful use of available time to opti-
mize planning and preparation throughout the organization.

But be careful when planning. Taking more time
to plan often results in better synchronization; *however*, any delay in execution risks yielding the initiative—with more time to prepare and act—to the enemy or, in the private and public sectors, to the
competition.

This does not negate the need for deliberation
and due diligence.

Instead, planning should reinforce them and
bring them to the forefront of any consideration.
When allocating planning time to the staff, Commanders must ensure that subordinates have
enough time to plan and organize their actions before execution. Commanders follow the *one-third—
two-thirds rule* to allocate time.

They allocate one-third of the available time to
execute their planning and distribute the remaining
two-thirds to their subordinates for planning and
preparation.[36] This time is critical because it includes rehearsals. These rehearsals hone and refine
skills, streamlining synchronization processes
across sections and departments. By extension, it involves taking care of your people—the team.

By providing the time for your subordinate
teammates to rehearse, you provide the foundation
that Dubik alluded to: trust, confidence, and training, whose trial results are lives saved.

Rehearsals are also intended for all participants
to ask questions if the plan is ambiguous. If there
are joint partners, they can slap the table with the
hosting units to confirm the plan before leaving the

rehearsals. Instead of being a talk-through method for tasks that depend on other synchronized efforts, the rehearsals are a combined, physically interactive procedure.

Each key player walks and talks their role across and around an operational map, synchronizing points, critical decisions, and triggers that drive other operations.

A key objective is for participants to interact with and learn from one another in a simulated, real-time setting. As such, they obtain situational awareness of the more extensive operation and grasp their roles and impact.

The same is plausible in a collaborative partnership for product development or product launch in the private sector. Over time, the format can morph into what suits the organization; it does not have to be perfect from its genesis.

A process is a series of actions or operations that lead to a specific outcome.[37] That end must include trust in the leader. Trust that the leader will step up and make the right decision in any scenario—your process's successes hinge on confidence in the culture and, more importantly, the leader.

Despite establishing a culture where single points of failure are discouraged, the military does not relieve you of your responsibility.

The leader is responsible for everything.

They may delegate their authority in the developmental process and during problem-solving by giving subordinates some autonomy of action.

Yet, the responsibility is still solely theirs. Right, wrong, or indifferent.

"The soldier, above all other people, prays for peace, for he must suffer and bear the deepest wounds and scars of war."
Douglas MacArthur

The MDMP and TLP in Action

You have read, watched, and heard enough *war stories*. However, there are never too many because good people do their jobs daily. The difference in what you are about to read is that these *everyday events* occur in unique situations.

Reacting and sometimes doing their jobs for each other, their country, and the flag during these unique situations, and how they handled them, are what make them exceptional.

The leaders you are about to meet, like the five I mentioned earlier, would tell you that nothing they did was exceptional or anything other than *us doing our jobs.*

The takeaway is how uniquely tied to our processes our team's successes were. They were achieved through cohesive collaboration, building strong, loyal, trusted, dependable bonds, and executing plans built on the MDMP and TLPs.

"Charger 3-2, this is Truck 4 over!"

"Truck 4, Charger 3-2, go!"

"Yeah, Roger 3-2, I see a kid up here with what looks like a spool, and he's paying out what looks like wire over!"

The early years of the Iraq invasion during Operation Iraqi Freedom were filled with crude Improvised Explosive Devices. They ranged from stuffed dead animal carcasses and soda cans to trash and tires, including water jugs.

Anything could be altered and hidden, especially if it seemed mundane and blended with the surroundings. Using children in the placement of these crude devices was not unheard of as a tactic. One of our processes for addressing this threat was to *pass* the potential target to the next vehicle to determine the best Positive Identification (PID).

Identification, in our context, means seeing a weapon tied to your perception of a hostile act that made you feel threatened. Specifically, during combat, the Rules of Engagement (RoE) regarding PID were *that if you had a reasonable certainty that the observed target was, in fact, a legitimate military target,* you could engage.

To a young mind, this statement must be enforced and codified by more patient, experienced, and diligent leaders. These leaders are armed only with the expectation of making better judgments and, in this case, the unwanted *luxury* of *having done this before* and being expected to be correct.

This is another reason the final decision-makers lose their fidelity to deciding without this due process, especially when no one is taking it back.

Thus, alleviating single points of failure is so important. However, this came with one significant risk inherent in it. What if we were wrong when the first observer reported and did nothing about it? The kid could pull the trigger if it were. Or his spotter, often time hidden as an actual trigger, could.

However, we were also on edge, which made things even more interesting.

"Stand-by Truck 4."

"Gun 2... (a truck equipped with a mounted weapon and gunner); *this is 3-2; what do you see over?"*

"Roger 3-2, I see the same as Truck 4; he seems to be feeding the wire from his waist over!"

"Attention on the net, this is Charger 3-2. Everyone ensures we hold our fire and maintain our tactical patience; let's give this kid a chance to prove himself...!"

Everyone responded appropriately, but I knew tensions were running high. Based on my experience in Operation Desert Storm in 1990, I had socialized to the team some expectations of what busy Middle Eastern City centers could look like before deployment.

Baghdad was no different. We were pushing convoys through the city in broad daylight, during the week, and during market hours.

Children were bound to be present, and their behavior of running alongside convoys with things in their hands was a part of the landscape.

It does not matter whether your process is short or lengthy. What matters is that everyone knows.

The simplicity of action trumps complicated, cumbersome processes. Why have a process that wastes resources and time yet fails to produce the desired results? I told you before I am no fan of cliches, but *the old definition of insanity* is appropriate here.

Right about this time, my vehicle, with a mounted gun and gunner, approaches where the kid is spotted.

I can see him.

Using just the internal vehicle communications to my driver, I said, *"Hey! Slow it down some."* To my gunner, *"Nice and slow, come up above defilade, tell me what you see."* This technique, which we used during convoys and patrols, was aptly nicknamed *'name-tape defilade.'*

The gunner's body was *exposed* only above the spot on their uniform where their name tape was aligned with the top of the vehicle and further protected by armor.

Gunner, *"Roger."*

Simultaneously, we both said aloud what we had made out. Both of us were half laughing. *"Goddamn it, man, It's a cassette tape!"*

Immediately, I keyed the radio receiver and said, *"Attention on the net. Be advised that the kid only has a busted cassette tape with the tape flailing out. Stand down, 3-2 out!"*

I agree that every situation has obstacles and variables. However, the impetus at the center of any change initiative is the people, the spokes in the wheel that create balance, eliminate drag, and increase production through performance.

I shared the previous incident not because of its outcome or the event itself, but because I wanted to emphasize our trust in each other and our equipment to execute what needed to be done.

They were built and anchored on our mutual values, beliefs, training, team, and, by extension, processes. It needed to be that way.

We were entering Iraq for what was to be a long year, and luckily, there were no shots fired in that event.

These processes may seem easy or routine, but for them to work, leaders must set the conditions early and reassess the plan, performance, and setbacks often during operations.

Throughout the operations process, Commanders, subordinate commanders, staff, and unified action partners collaborate, sharing and questioning information, beliefs, and ideas to understand situations and make decisions.

The Commander fosters a learning environment through collaboration, enabling participants to think critically and creatively, and share their thoughts, opinions, and recommendations without fear of reprimand.[38]

So, can CEOs, managers, department heads, and leaders do the same? The results of creating such an environment equate to critical and creative thinking that extends from planning cells to action on the ground.

The MDMP can be integrated into operations, enabling subordinates to execute missions in real-time without waiting for follow-on orders.

But to earn that autonomy of action, there must be the kind of trust we spoke about in Chapters One and Six. It can be daunting to be charged with caring for the well-being of America's sons and daughters, especially those who are in combat.

I suspect that private-sector workplaces have similar challenges. To put it simply, careful consideration must be given to selecting and placing influential individuals with relevant training, experience, and vetted leadership experience at critical decision-making points.

It is vital to success.

Two years later, in the same battle space as in 2004.

"Mustang 3-2, Viper 2, over."

"Viper 2, go for 3-2 over."

"Be advised, I have a car at a high rate of speed not responding to signals over."

"How far out, over?"

"3-2, roughly 300-350 meters (about the height of the Empire State Building), *and traveling fast, over."*

In the early years of the war, some standard Techniques, Tactics, and Procedures (TTP), such as tactical patience in operating military vehicles in heavily populated civilian areas, had not been fully developed. They were a work in progress, based on the enemy's current situation and their procedures.

To address the issue of deterring them from approaching our vehicles to avoid incidents, the brass considered several options. One of them was using a series of signals that were time-of-day dependent. If it were dark, we would use lasers and lights to attract the vehicle's attention and cause it to slow down or back off. The government of Iraq was supposed to disseminate this information, including minimal following distances and other processes adopted by both governments throughout the country.

Flags, hand signals, weapon pointing, and yelling were available during daylight hours. At the time, the standoff distance was 150 meters (about half the height of the Empire State Building) or greater. Warning shots, followed by a kill shot, were the final options.

Another consideration this time was the new sophistication in IEDs coupled with the recent madness of Vehicle Borne Improvised Explosive Devices or VBIEDs. These were vehicles either driven or strategically parked, loaded to the gills with explosive charges and leftover artillery rounds thrown about the country, or still accessible by rogue militant factions of Saddam Hussein's Baath Party.

"Viper 2, you have tried lights and lasers, Roger?"

"Roger that 3-2, he's still coming." "Roger Viper 2, send signals again rapidly, over." "Roger 3-2."

I knew an Iraqi police checkpoint was about six clicks (about 3.5 miles) ahead. If we can hold him off until the checkpoint, we could use the police to translate our intentions. I used this TTP once before, and it worked.

A comparable situation had arisen several weeks earlier: we were *bird-dogged* by a car in identical nighttime conditions. Using lasers and flags, we reached a checkpoint, where I had my Assistant Convoy Commander socialize with the police to hold the car there, give us a two-mile head start, and explain the policy.

I intended that if the police clarified the instructions, and after being permitted to go, the car insisted on the behavior, our options would be much more fluid.

His intentions were not nefarious. We saw his lights at an acceptable distance for the better part of our patrol. *"Mustang 3-2, Viper 2, over."*

"Send it over."

"Roger, he's still bearing down with no intent to slow down over." "Distance now, over?"

*"Less than 200 meters (this is now about twice
the height of the Statue of Liberty), over."*
*"OK, Roger. Send the lights again in combination. If
he is still coming, fire a warning shot driver-side away."*
"Roger that over!"

Viper 2 had indicated in other traffic that he
could see passengers in the car. That was the decision for the driver's side and away. In the worst-
case scenario, we would still neutralize the threat
and minimize collateral damage if he misses.

In the base case, he sees the muzzle flash and
hears the explosive sound of the M2 Machine Gun
that they are known to have, then slows down and
backs off.

Any rational person will stop unless they are determined to pursue a different cause. However, as I
indicated in Chapter One, all good plans often blow
up in your face at the point of departure.

"Mustang 3-2, Viper 2, a warning shot fired over."
"Status of Vic… (short for vehicle) *… now over?"*
"Uhm, Roger, he is stopped but on fire over!"
"Say again! Over! "
"Roger 3-2, the Vic is engulfed in flames, over!"
"This is 3-2. Halt the convoy now!" After halting, I
reconfirmed our security posture and sent the fol-
lowing.

*"Attention on the net. This is 3-2; everyone keeps their
heads on a swivel. Do your 5s and 25s and be alert."*

"Mustang 3-3 (the Assistant Convoy Commander), *3-2 over."*

"Send 3-2; this is 3-3."

"Break! Break! Break! (This communication technique interrupts normal traffic for priority traffic.)

Hey, 3-2, this is Viper 2; now I have dismounts from the car heading into the sand over!" "Descriptions?"

"Looks like two women and an older man over."

The sinking feeling of *"this is not what we thought it was"* starts to creep in. You start wondering whether everyone is out of the vehicle, which by now was fully engulfed.

As part of our process, during security halts, everyone enters a mode triggered by the event. Security gun trucks are oriented to protect the convoy from all angles and possible opportunistic attacks.

Individual drivers and assistant drivers conduct what we call 5s and 25s. It is a system in which you visually scan between the numbers and repeat the process. In doing so, we would spot potential IEDs by seeing explosives, wires, and anything outside the ordinary.

The designated medical vehicle is awaiting clearance *to proceed* to the point of injury to treat any casualties. Recovery vehicles, if needed, await the same measures to recover. In this instance, there is no need for recovery. We could not have recovered an Iraqi vehicle without prior coordination and permission. I met my Assistant Commander already on the sand with the car's occupants and the interpreter. As I walked over, I could see the occupants: an older gentleman, an older lady, a younger lady, and a *baby*.

As in a baby who was still nursing!

Angry and exasperated, I asked, *"Why?"* After spending much more time asking and answering the same question through the interpreter, we left them several cases of *Meals Ready to Eat* (MREs), the meals we eat, and several cases of water.

I gave them the contact slip we carried in our dispatches for situations where we encountered citizens with concerns, bid them peace and farewell, and were on our way.

Apart from many *"I..., we... love America"* and a feeble translation of something about a vacation and the city of Mosul, we never entirely understood the reason. We discussed leaders being responsible for everything related to their teammates. Those responsibilities include their mental and spiritual health, which are intricately aligned and considered throughout the MDMP's initial planning stages. Considerations include the placement of Chaplains to provide religious services, counsel, and other services.

So far, you have read the down-trail user-level results of a larger operational plan. A plan that required our success, like all the others, to give us the edge and be successful. All these minor *battles*, collectively, we believed, would ultimately result in our winning the war.

I know my gunner was not the same, knowing how close his shot came to killing a family.

We later speculated that the bullet had hit the car's fuel tank.

But how could he have known?

How could any of us?

Many of our teammates visited the Chaplain after that patrol to recalibrate.

I did, too.

I still feel better today that our systems worked despite a near miss and a burnt-out Chevrolet Impala in Iraq.

The event's results were not due to artful skill and complex moves.

They worked because our teams worked. Our people worked. Not because they were exceptional to anyone else. But internally, we were unique to ourselves. We highly regard human life and its sanctity, cherishing it. Even if some are determined to kill us, even among those lives, we value life. We will do everything required to preserve it—our processes and decision-making mandates. Our leaders depended on us to carry out the MDMP's decisions, act rationally, and display due diligence in our actions. Cynics will think otherwise, but the truth is that America knows.

—

We implemented a new process during Operation Iraqi Freedom and Operation Enduring Freedom in Iraq and Afghanistan, respectively. That plan was to embed reporters with deployed units, specifically frontline units. We were not all fans of the idea, at least not at first. The premise behind the decision was full disclosure. Show what America's sons and daughters were capable of. Show our military might with our people behind these powerful weapons and systems, and remove the negative cloud that can form over a large-scale military operation.

Unlike Vietnam, where numerous questions, doubts, and speculations surrounded America's military actions, this move aimed to clarify and dispel those concerns, in addition to the ones mentioned above. I worried that simple mission nuances could be misconstrued and reported negatively, tarnishing the military's reputation or, worse yet, further complicating relationships and operations based on their reporting.

They were reporters who, rightly or wrongly, were perceived as unfriendly to war efforts and disliked by soldiers.

Or so went the misconception. In retrospect, the idea was a near-genius move. And when it comes to full disclosure, there was plenty of disillusionment to clarify.

We needed wins.

We needed the American people to understand that our processes work when they can be executed using the right leaders.

Abu Ghraib was our anomaly.

It was, and still is, a gut punch that leaves you winded because it went against so many good things—like events in the Vietnam Conflict in which the ugly always took center stage, rightly or wrongly, so did Abu Ghraib. It initially robbed us of credibility and momentum, like Lamb's predicament, but in a different way.

We needed to level the bubble and win for us and our Vietnam-era brothers and sisters.

I felt so.

I have never participated in, heard of, or seen an order that implied or outright stated a violation of the Geneva Convention.

That does not mean that truths aren't distorted, lies are told, and the human psyche, albeit often good, can become evil and nefarious. Worst yet, it is condoned by single-point-of-failure leadership.

For those reasons, the media's embedded reporters were necessary, and we needed wins, as I said earlier. The hope was that a relationship would be built on and around symbiosis. We need them to tell our stories, and they need us to have stories to tell.

With innovative technologies, new and diverse ideologies, and revised policies towards war and global conflicts, we can rectify some of our teammates' mistakes by emphasizing the actions we are taking on the ground, where collateral damage situations and decisions arise.

The world, but more importantly, at home, could see the deliberate planning, the influx of information and recommendations provided by people, and the struggles sometimes faced by decision-makers in making those decisions.

We needed wins like these to maintain the momentum.

We found one in Karl Zinsmeister.

Former White House Domestic Policy Council Director, researcher, and reporter embedded with the 82nd Airborne in Iraq wrote in his book *Boots on the Ground,*[39]

"The real story of the Iraq War thus far, I suggest, has been the leverage the U.S. military has foregone, not the leverage it has applied. Our leaders have been shooting for the hearts and minds of everyday Iraqis as much as for the gangsters of the Baath party, and military officers have willingly fought with their hands tied in the interest of sparing civilians. Anyone who tells the world otherwise is plain wrong."

He was referring to his observation of a mission being executed in real-time. That mission, in short, was to take out a structure with known bad players inside. Still, because of the proportionality of the weapon's decision to minimize collateral damage, targets escaped, and, as Zinsmeister observed, the Commanding General's comments after the fact, *"Looks like we needed a bigger punch."*

Yes, tactical patience is partly due to the intelligence available and the emotional intelligence of the decision-maker. But more importantly, these backstops, or *no-go* decision points, are not accidental. They were rigorously debated, discussed, and, in some cases, even rehearsed.

Again, so much depends on their being right the first time. Yet again, this is another example of the process's benefits. Remember, there are no resets or do-overs in combat.

Yes, even if this temperance is not in our favor or beneficial to the plan, we are charged to be temperate. Even when we are frustrated and tired, and situations seem overwhelming, we are charged to be temperate.

I admit I did not follow Zinsmeister's reporting during or after my tours in Iraq. The truth is, until I conducted research, I did not know who he was, but I am glad for individuals like him who are honest in their observations and criticisms.

I hope those who watched and read him included some of our teammates from the Vietnam Conflict.

They needed to read and hear things like Zinsmeister's candid observations.

They deserve it.

Best Practices to Section II

Set conditions in which the team trusts each other and themselves. Develop these through repetition, evaluation, and assessment.

Understand that a team has no "I" and that this is not just a cliché or an extraordinary statement. Instead, it is significant in its practical meaning and application. Remember that as the leader, you set conditions for and drive whatever procedures your establishment uses. You are also charged with encouraging and emphasizing team collaboration. Stove-piping information is dangerous, counterproductive, and counterintuitive.

Develop processes, such as utilizing knowledge managers armed with knowledge management systems, to capture, store, and share lessons learned and best practices. The Abu Ghraib incident was a disgrace and a textbook lesson in poor leadership. It is a sore topic for soldiers still serving who were aware of the incidents. It is a painful subject for veterans, too, maybe because it ran counter to what we were trying to achieve. A few bad apples did not represent our culture and placed our processes under scrutiny. Some warranted, and others not.

These leaders are single points of failure, not necessarily a broken system. When this occurs, individuals should be immediately removed from the culture through other organizational systems. Then, build corrective training and workshops into your operations.

Remember that although you can delegate authority, you are responsible for everyone and everything in your sphere of influence and responsibility. In other words, you cannot delegate your responsibility. Build easily understood and navigable systems. Ensure everyone is familiar with the procedures and quickly reassess, refine, and disseminate the refinements.

Chapter 8

"Criticism of the system is often an elegant alibi to downgrade the individual's responsibility."
Niko Paech

A Social Experiment

The dictionary provides several definitions for the term "system." One uses the word *things* to unite with others to accomplish something. We will use the more appropriate set of principles or procedures according to which something is done, such as an organized framework or method.[40] I said 'more appropriately' because procedures are consistent with processes and principles and demonstrate a sense of ownership. A system's principles are the foundation for its beliefs and how it will function inherently.

We briefly discussed age and demographics in Chapter Four, but I want to examine all these factors and others within the scope of systems. This will also highlight the level of detail and consideration given to the human element during the MDMP, particularly in the garrison setting. For years, society has been navigating the delicate balance between social responsibility and fulfilling the needs of their cities and states, guided by political and, now more than ever, social mandates.

Addressing this is urgently needed in the private and public sectors today. Corporations provide more modern, aesthetically, ergonomically, environmentally, and socially conscious workplaces, but this is often insufficient.

As I write this, businesses struggle to find unique solutions to these issues, such as hybrid workdays and remote work options, or not requiring a physical workplace. These are just a few of the remedies that have been implemented and are still being refined.

The military is no different in balancing these issues. Except physically, not being at work is not an option. A no-collaborative workplace, one that avoids physical contact, runs a significantly higher risk of failure.

Without insulting anyone's intellect, it is implausible that a military context would not have an in-person workforce due to its purpose and readiness requirements. However, that did not deter the military from flexing its muscles.

During the early onset of the COVID-19 pandemic, the Army had to adapt to maintain readiness by transitioning to hybrid workplaces similar to those I mentioned earlier.

Like the public and private sectors, the military has systems. They have a myriad of them. Some systems play a role in deterrence, offense, and defense. Others collect and analyze; on the other hand, there are those internal to individual units per their mission requirements and daily battle rhythm events.

This is not accidental.

Not at all.

Putting aside the primary role of deterrence for a moment, let us explore those systems that are more designed and tailored to take care of people.

I struggled with using the phrase 'social experiment' as the subheading for this chapter because of its negative connotations.

Then I thought, not so when it is used in this context.

At least, I do not think so.

Where else can you find a more diverse group of people in the same place, living and working closely together for an exceptionally long time every day?

Without a doubt, the answer is the military.

—

With that in mind, let's anchor the conversations around an entry I read in the *International Encyclopedia of the Social and Behavioral Sciences (2001, p. 41).*

The author made a powerful argument for the military as a social, psychological, and experimental proving ground.

I want to expand on his thesis as a point of departure for our discussion of systems. However, before doing so, I must state vehemently that I disagree with the military as a social experiment.

"It does not matter how beautiful your theory is; it does not matter how smart you are. If it does not agree with experiment, it is wrong."
Richard P. Feynman

When socially and politically correct trends grab the attention of democratically free societies, the government-controlled military system often functions as society's social-psychological experimental laboratory.

The military is a closed-loop system in which uniformed personnel belong to and work for their military bosses 24 hours a day, 365 days a year. J.P. Kreuger, a Social Psychologist and author of the broader thesis and idea behind the findings, characterized the military as a social experiment. It is also why the MDMP plays a crucial role in the decision-making process.

The decisions derived from its process are often life-altering or changing. Kreuger's theory is correct in part. I say partly because the same is inaccurate in garrison, despite being true in combat. Soldiers understand that they are *on duty* 24 hours a day, seven days a week, should their unit or the nation call them.

However, when in garrison and not otherwise scheduled on a task, soldiers are home at night and on weekends with their families.

This is true for both active and reserve components of all branches. Remember transformation, and transforming? There was a time when Kreuger's assessment was accurate in its entirety.

In the 1990s, when I enlisted, and even before my service, soldiers spent an average of thirty days per quarter training on their skills in a *field setting*.

They packed all their tactical equipment and personal gear and *deployed to* the training area, artfully nicknamed *The Box*. This Box was sometimes at the installation to which they were assigned, sometimes in another part of the state, or even in another state entirely. They would stay in this setting for the duration of the exercise. They were disconnected from their families and the *world*, except in times of emergency.

The same applies to combat in emergencies, where operational requirements permit. Kreuger's essay provided five examples that will guide our discussion.

He stipulates, *"integrating the workforce through an influx of members of all religions, racial and ethnic minorities, women, and, more recently, gay people and instituting sexual harassment awareness and other sensitivity training in the workplace."* So far, everything is accurate, and the successes prove it.

He continued, *"Implementing tobacco-smoking cessation, control of recreational drugs and alcohol use, family advocacy programs, personal weight control, physical fitness, and uniform dress regulations."*

Overall, the Army and the military continue to work through these issues, from congressionally mandated changes to common-sense initiatives geared toward transformation and chaired by each branch.

There's more, *"Adoption of the British Army's regimental unit replacement personnel transfer policies whereby a whole military unit's personnel, and dependent families, relocate together as a group from one military assignment to another."*

The last two points — dress regulations and reassignments — were significant changes.

This is significant because, in some respects, the changes were immediate. Krueger says, *"Making it mandatory for military personnel to subject themselves to inoculations, experimental drugs, and therapeutics, or, owing to insufficient supplies, withholding drug treatments for some personnel.*"[43] Because of the prolonged stays away from families, including the wars in Afghanistan and Iraq, there was a noticeable increase in relationship issues.

Divorces were on the rise.

Both physical and mental abuse were also on the rise. Substance and alcohol abuse permeated the forces. So, too, was the number of suicides.

The *RAND Center for Military Health Policy Research* stated that increasing suicides among military members raised concern among policymakers, military leaders, and the population.[44]

Something had to be done.

The military complex had to address this influx of family and individual problems. The numbers are just too staggering.

—

In 2011, in *The War Within, Preventing Suicide in the U.S. Military,* a study by the *RAND* Institute reported that the suicide rate across the DoD has been climbing, rising from 10.3 in 2001 to 15.8 in 2008, representing about a 50-percent increase. 50 percent! That is half in seven years! It may seem long to some, but contextually, it is a concise time window. This increase in the DoD suicide rate is attributable to a doubling of the pace in the Army.

Again, the military had to put its decision-making process to work.

There is evidence that the suicide rate in the DoD in the calendar year 2007 was higher than in the calendar years 2001 and 2002. There is also evidence that 2008 was higher than the annual rate between 2001 and 2005 and higher than the average rate for calendar years 2001 through 2008.[45] As I said, these are alarmingly high numbers. Some could argue that despite these numbers, causation may not indicate a correlation between leadership and decision-making. The study's results would dispute that thinking.

One of the many things they advocated for was *responding appropriately,* along with other *best practices* such as increasing time at home with families and several other recommendations that included treatment and care.

I suspect responding appropriately was a call to action for leaders. Leaders had to make the most of the time they had allocated for training by maximizing their efforts. To Kreuger's point, families, as a rule, traveled together on most reassignment moves.

These changes placed the onus on commanders and initiated a significant shift in the exposure of individuals with and without emotional intelligence.

Emotional Intelligence

These, like the stories that came before them and those to follow, are the results of the MDMP being used again to solve complex issues.

Remember our discussion on best practices regarding our impatience with some of the decisions we have implemented? I suspect that, coupled with not knowing such a process existed until reading this, and unless otherwise militarily associated, these factors may contribute to why it may seem new.

Change is a catalyst for everyone involved. On that account, a principled outcome must be dependent on patience. So, for the cynics who would say *"a little too late,"*

I say, *"Better late than never."*

You see, your decisions are driven by your perceptions of what you encounter. Ask yourself, *"Are you a glass half full or half empty person?"* The answer to that question will help you understand why you made certain decisions.

As humans, we have taboos about anything, from using otherwise discarded parts of animals for food to plants for medicinal reasons and the body as art in our religious beliefs and practices.

—

"Hey, Sergeant P, got a minute?" asked one of my squad leaders while walking toward me.

"Sure. What's going on?" I asked, leading us into our office space.

"Specialist Dean wants to schedule an appointment with the Chaplain."

"For?"

"Oh, nothing bad. She wants to see if he can get her somewhere private to worship." We spoke briefly about Chaplains earlier. Let's highlight them here. Chaplains facilitate worship services and other counseling and mentorship services within their units.

Services include scheduling a suitable location and setup and then providing aid if required during the worship services. This is despite most Chaplains being clergy in their specific denomination or faith.

In other words, their role is to promote spirituality and dedication, serving all service members and their families, regardless of their background or religion. The uniqueness of the request was the religion Dean practiced. Dean practiced Wicca. *"That's a new one,"* I said in ignorance.

"Never heard of it either until she told me during a counseling session," he said. *"Let me get back to you; I'm sure Chappy can figure something out,"* I promised, picking up the phone.

According to religioustolerance.org, Wicca is the largest Neopagan religion in the U.S. and other Western countries. Wiccans revere the Earth, their Goddess, and her consort, the Horned God. Their primary rule of behavior is the Wiccan Rede, which prohibits them from harming others, including themselves, except in cases of self-defense or when necessary to protect others.[46]

Chappy came through, of course, and Specialist Dean was able to worship. But some may ask, *"What was so significant about the event?"*

Or better yet, how does it relate to problem-solving and the Military decision-making process? The answer is that it exposes and illuminates what I mentioned about Sep and emotionally intelligent leaders and leadership.

Imagine a scenario in which it would have been more accessible and beneficial if Chappy, an Orthodox by religious grouping, had dismissed the request on many grounds, should he have felt that the teachings went against or clashed with his beliefs. No one would be the wiser.

Wicca was not well known to us then—or at least not to me. Although it is the largest Neopagan religion in the West, it is not often discussed or included in the mainstream. She could have been ridiculed and made to feel out of place.

The instruments of her worship could have given way to disdain, contempt, and even harassment. They are not mainstream and would be seen as taboo.

Our team was young and still working through the daily compromises of living, working, understanding each other, and serving together in a hostile environment. Emotionally intelligent leaders consider these factors in their decisions, even when the decisions do not win favor with everyone. Ultimately, they benefit the team. Those were not the only variables.

At the time, we were deployed in Iraq. Facility space and privacy were not at a premium, and the Chaplain's schedule was packed with dealing with other deployment issues in the country and back home in the United States.

He, like the rest of us, had to prioritize his time. And without sounding crass, what was the harm if he could not find the time for one soldier?

Absolutely! There could be harmful repercussions.

Remember, we spoke earlier about the concept of whole-soldier readiness? We noted that spiritual readiness, along with the others we laid out, was a factor. Therefore, although this event is nuanced, it goes to the more prominent theme of the team as a sum of its parts. It is also easy to argue that it is the charge and expectations of a Chaplain to do the right thing. His religious teachings mandated that he act honorably, ethically, and Godly.

As the spiritual advisor in the unit, he was an example, so of course, he worked on the request—all true.

But what if it is more than that? What if, to my point, it is the interplay between team members and each understanding the value of the other? These emotionally intelligent leaders know that no matter how insignificant a teammate's input may seem, it must not be ignored. All intake matters. It is the commander's prerogative to consider them and then discard them.

They cannot be treated as afterthoughts. Each team member's value is another brick in building collaborative, cohesive, solid teams. As a result, these leaders recognize this interplay and act accordingly.

Emotionally intelligent leaders, especially those with well-developed interpersonal and empathy skills, are more likely to appreciate the impact of their behavior. They are also more likely to care about the consequences.[47]

More of this phenomenon will be displayed soon, and its interplay with their understanding of what is essential to the people working in their organizations and society[48] will become known.

EI leaders tend to be more engaging because people can relate to them; they will feel more accessible, inspire trust, and better understand what is considered fair. Therefore, developing emotionally intelligent leaders is crucial to developing ethical organizations.[49]

As a part of our convoy processes, the Chaplain was given a block of time when he was available to read scripture, fellowship, and pray with us before we departed on missions.

When we returned, the same was true. Chappy would greet the convoys with cold, refreshing goodies we called *lickies and chewies*. In his truck, the Chaplain's Assistant carried a large cooler filled with sodas, water, Gatorade, and a caffeine-laden drink called *Ripits*.

The soldiers craved those and the numerous types of candy, especially after patrols. The heat was sometimes unforgiving, and wearing all our required gear worsened it.

This small gesture and making it back alive from our patrols made the world suitable again, just for a while.

It was not just Chappy's responsibility to facilitate Dean's spiritual well-being. It was fair to her and, by extension, to the unit and team. Fairness in and of itself is crucial. The perception of fairness is equally important.

Studies show that perceptions of fairness are associated with positive emotions and attitudes, such as higher organizational commitment, as well as with positive behaviors, including strong corporate citizenship.

Conversely, perceptions of unfairness are related to negative emotions and attitudes, such as organizational cynicism, as well as negative behaviors, including withdrawal and antisocial acts.

Moreover, the adverse effects of unfairness are more vital than the positive effects of fairness. The impact of nonuniformity is consistent with the well-established phenomenon of negative imprinting in human perception and judgment, which has been consistently demonstrated in numerous studies.

We must also tell them often when they get it right. Emotionally intelligent leaders know this.

—

"Pennicooke! How often should you counsel?"

"Every month, Sergeant Major!" I answered smartly.

"Wrong stud!" he bellowed, walking down the hall.

"You counsel every freakin' time it's warranted!"

Have you heard of or seen those crusty old Command Sergeant Majors that make you cringe?

He was one of those.

But, like Sep, Shot, Trump, Level, and Sergeant Major G, he was a leader and an expert in his craft.

His answer and explanation have stuck with me since. The rationale was even more profound.

"How often have we made sure we documented an event in which a teammate, particularly subordinates, came up short?" he continued.

He was right.

Some leaders often cannot wait to highlight their teammates' or subordinates' errors.

"Almost always," I responded, feeling guilty.

I was guilty because I had done that as a junior leader.

"Right? And rightfully so," he agreed. *"The bad behaviors or poor performance cannot be ignored and left unaddressed,"* he said. *"But, if I asked you when was the last time you, just in passing, praised a teammate or subordinate for executing something spontaneously and unexpectedly, but value-added, what would you say?"*

To say he stumped me is an understatement because, up to that moment, I was under the correct yet incomplete belief that counseling and mentorship only had to occur monthly or if a significant event happened during the month's activities. In other words, I thought it was a formality.

Mind you, there is nothing wrong with the monthly formal counseling. But to the Command Sergeant Major's point, every day, every opportunity is one in which leaders can mentor, coach, counsel, and teach.

Furthermore, it is an effective way to receive *real-time* feedback on the progress of things. This informal mentoring and counseling meeting can be a single episode, as the Command Sergeant Major suggests, or an ongoing engagement.

It can be as simple as when you talked to someone who gave you an insight that influenced *your*
career.

Interestingly, these episodes are more likely to
occur if you become genuinely open to mentoring
moments. When people feel genuinely cared for
and about, they are more inclined to open up and
share their insights, issues, and concerns.

These can strengthen the bonds of trust and open
communication channels, a significant consideration of readiness.

—

Given the demands placed on them through service, you may ask why service members serve.
Some do because it is a family tradition.

Great-grandfathers and grandfathers served, and
so too did their offspring.

Some seek opportunities that remove them from
difficult lifestyle choices and decisions, while others
serve for various reasons.

However, I have observed that once the initial
itch has been scratched, regardless of one's pedi-
gree, some members do not want to leave and, as
such, make careers out of their service.

Cynics would disagree, arguing that the military
serves as a financial and social welfare outlet and
safety net for those who would otherwise be finan-
cially insecure. I must disagree with that premise.
Even if the assumption is initially valid, the sacrifice
and effort produced by these people far surpass the
pay.

I mentioned anomalies earlier, and I will concede that among the servant leaders I am focused on, some stray, lose their way, and often fall short of their own goals, as well as those of the organization. What is significant is that the team will still rally to their side.

It is not always because their creed stipulates that they leave no one behind.

Instead, it reinforces the notion that a deviation from the values and norms that make the institution—the system—requires and needs their efforts to be whole.

Sometimes, we must lose our way to find our purpose, and leaders must be willing to recognize that.

That is quintessentially the difference between the military and the public sector. The military addresses problems by identifying and resolving the root causes, utilizing the Military Decision-Making Process (MDMP).

They do not give a false sense of, '*Oh, just a rough patch; we'll be okay,*' and sweep the benign and insignificant issues under the rug.

There are ways to right a wrong without denigrating, belittling, and mistreating people to get results. Or jeopardize your integrity by prioritizing *someone's feelings* over a prudent decision.

Remember Captain Trump?

He dealt with the issue, remember?

It is also why choosing with whom these decisions rest and those advising decision-makers is critical. There is too much riding on the outcomes for it not to be that way. In the service, some nuances of training exist, including the unique techniques used by Drill Sergeants and instructors to break down civilians and mold them into soldiers. Still, those are the exceptions, not the rule.

That is necessary and not in the context to which I am referring. I have often counseled my soldiers and encouraged peers to place themselves in the shoes of someone who has lost their way.

You do not continue to pressure the teammate, assuming they already feel inadequate because of their error. This tactic prevents people from reaching out and opening up to others, which is critical to readiness. More importantly, it is crucial to take care of people.

Address the problem, not the person. This is where emotionally intelligent leaders thrive. It is built on that innate urge to serve.

You will soon find that as you begin to act, your consciousness evolves into leadership. My final assessment of servant leaders (those who prioritize the well-being of others and those being served) is that military personnel shift their mindset from an autocratic focus on self-interest to a more servant-leader approach.

The German philosopher Emmanuel Kant would likely agree, as this approach embodies his broader philosophy, in which people view themselves as purposefully aligned with the betterment of those around them.

As such, the symbiosis necessary for such a relationship to thrive requires this alignment. This is not just for the service members but also for government contractors working with them.

In my job, things are constantly changing. Nothing is ever static or completely fluid.

I recall conducting an internal After-Action Review (AAR) for our analysts' team. We discussed how our reporting and systems were working and agreed that they were not.

There were gaps in the flow of information, and the top-down, bottom-up refinement was cumbersome.

During one of our training exercises, where we gathered data on the training unit, a *real-world* injury occurred. In civilian speak, that is a severe incident involving injury during training.

Tracking and reporting these incidents is one of our responsibilities.

The incident occurred early in the morning, and the complete report and information collection were not finished and accurate until late that afternoon. It was clear that the system was broken. In our base case, we hoped it was a single point of failure that we could quickly find and remedy.

That was not the case. The issues were more profound than we first thought. The decision to change our reporting format was immediate, given the high potential for related results. Therefore, the organization needed to improve efficiency, and the procedures it had implemented had to be reworked.

To achieve this, incremental change aims to enhance the internal alignment between existing organizational components, enabling them to operate

more effectively and improve the organization's efficiency. However, this approach would not be
practical in this case, given the urgency for change.

We would not have the luxury of incremental
change because of the severity of the incident and
its impact. It had to be immediate.

This change was not opposed, as it involved irre-
versible damage to the family and the individual
concerned. Typically, change recommendations are
met with resistance and a culture of inertia,[50,] but
not in this case.

We quickly implemented and disseminated the
changes among other teams to synchronize reporting efforts. Since its implementation, we have not
experienced any lags or misreporting in our re-
ports.

Most importantly, the implemented changes
will better serve the soldiers and their families in
the future, eliminating unnecessary emotional
stress on families during an already challenging
period in their lives.

—

To Kreuger's point on sexual orientation and behavior in the military, I remember the struggle during the *Don't Ask, Don't Tell* years that the lesbian
and gay soldier community went through.

I had soldiers who were both. They knew I
knew, and vice versa, but no words were ever spoken, as per the policy.

You may ask why, but even if there had been evidence of the behavior, I am unsure what my actions would have been. For me, the procedure was

never important. I also recognize the implications and questions that can arise from that position.

They were my people, and I did not *see* a difference when I saw them among their peers and battle buddies. They executed everything I asked of them. They never asked for special treatment. They never even implied it. Their character and contribution to the team were my mandate, not to judge affairs of the heart, at least not at first.

The government had set a framework or system for our work. The principles within that framework had to be based on the contributions and participation of everyone. That includes thinking critically, rationally, and creatively, stepping outside our insularities, and performing. I performed the first of those two predicates in many different settings; they did plenty of both, but more so the latter.

Kreuger's research highlighted problematic societal issues that are no longer isolated to everyday America. The military's insularity cannot protect it from the inevitable effects.

The effects of addiction were one such phenomenon we had to redress—addiction to illicit and prescription drugs, alcohol, and a combination of the three.

Not new to military behavior, mind you, but rampantly scarier, and the numbers, too, were climbing.

—

As I walked in, the First Sergeant said, *"It's an inconvenience, but it has to happen."* My entry had made everyone look around towards the door, and the First Sergeant continued sarcastically, *"Glad you could join us, Pennicooke!"*

I brushed aside the response I had in my head because he was the one who had called me and told me to get to his office as quickly as possible from the motor pool.

Considering the installation's traffic, I made it as quickly as possible.

Also, it was not the time or place to challenge the First Sergeant. There were more pressing issues, and being late was not the main event.

It was also petty.

For the past couple of months, we as a unit struggled with taking care of a teammate whom we had lost to illicit drug addiction.

After returning from deployment, Specialist Bell succumbed to the pressures of conflict and the changes upon return that so many go through, and to release the tensions, she became addicted.

We only found out through a concerned teammate who noticed the changes in her friend and reported her suspicions.

The military at the time did not have a drug addiction rehabilitation program. It had a program tailored around counseling, but nothing like the more robust civilian programs.

The Army's Substance and Abuse Prevention program, or ASAP, defines its approach as a *"clinical intervention to return Soldiers and other beneficiaries to full duty or identify Soldiers who are not able to be successfully rehabilitated."*

Treatment is deferred to the Defense Health Agency.

It requires command or self-referral and *"an in-depth individual biopsychosocial evaluation interview to determine if Soldiers and other beneficiaries need to be referred for treatment."* This is per Army Regulation 600-85, which governs the Army Substance Abuse Program.

With a zero-tolerance policy towards illicit drugs, there is no need for a more scripted, deliberate approach like that of the civilian sector, coupled with the policy that states, *"Abuse of alcohol, use of illegal drugs, and misuse of prescription drugs are inconsistent with Army values and the standards of performance, discipline, and readiness necessary to accomplish the Army's mission."*

I think it goes without much debate that service members are held to a higher standard of professionalism and mental acuity, ready and free from the effects of illicit drugs.

I know the chain of command struggled with how we helped the teammate and did not set new standards through our actions, despite having the directives of the DHA as tools.

Not to mention, navigating them is complicated by their wording.

Everyone, it seemed, had rallied to Bell's side as expected. And because of the cryptic nature of the First Sergeant's phone call, I suspected this was about Bell.

"Like I was saying, it looks like we found a program and a flight for Bell to Oakland, California, tomorrow," the First Sergeant continued.

"Hell yea, that's good shit!" said Bell's immediate supervisor, Staff Sergeant Rico. *"It is good shit,"* the

First Sergeant said, "the *problem is we need an escort to get her there."*

It was close to the Christmas holidays, so most soldiers had holiday leave requests and passes submitted to go home for the holidays.

"All of you have approved leave except you, Pennicooke, yes? he asked, already knowing the answers.

"Roger, First Sergeant," they all responded.

I was the only one quiet.

Looking at me with that *tag you're it* looks, he asked,

"Have any other plans?"

"No, First Sergeant," I said.

"Then it looks like you drew the short straw," he responded.

The inconvenience the First Sergeant had alluded to when I walked in was now heavier in the air.

I had no plans, but I also did not plan on an escorted trip to Oakland.

My trepidation was partly based on Specialist Bell's behavior when she needed her fix.

The soldier and teammate who would paint the sky if we asked her was almost unrecognizable in speech and appearance. She had a deep, gouged cut in her left calf, almost to the nerves, received from broken glass, trying to escape her room one night, trying to find a fix, which caused her to walk with crutches.

She had a dull, opaque look, and her cheeks were ghostly sunken, unattractively exposing her bone structure. Some of the things she would do and say back then saddened me.

After gathering all the details from the First Sergeant regarding flights, I left his office.

The flight was the next day.

After we arrived in Oakland, we took a taxi to the hotel. I checked us both in. I gave her the medication the hospital had given her to dull the pain in her leg and the one to take the edge off her need for a fix, and then I ordered us pizza. Partly because it was easy, and most significantly, it was containment.

My strategy was to have less exposure to the outside until morning, the better. I watched her dress her wound, eat the pizza, and chat up an incoherent storm until she fell asleep. I suspected the chattiness was a side effect of the drugs.

I did not sleep.

I was worried I would fall asleep; she would awaken, slip away, and be gone.

The thought of being *lost in Oakland, California, with an addiction* kept creeping into my thoughts.

The *check-in* process was a swift, surreal experience the following day.

I exchanged picture IDs with the point of contact I was given, shook hands, and introduced Bell to the counselor.

That was the first time I saw the weight of her circumstances come full circle. Tears welled up in her eyes as I hugged her and wished her well.

Inside, I was broken, too. For me, this was the last time I would see Specialist Bell. I was leaving the unit before the 90-day program's end.

Failing or succeeding, this was my final act. It was an emotionally charged moment because I also felt the weight of her circumstances. I was turning one of our own over to *strangers* to fix her.

I hated that we could not find an internal way to do it, but she promised to work hard on her rehabilitation.

I shook the counselor's hand and left. I later found out that Bell had completed the rehabilitation program. Sadly, the process ended her military career.

Still, as I last heard, she returned to Louisiana, met a good man, got married, and had two beautiful children.

It remains a mystery who the players were and how the plan led Bell into a program that saved her life. What is not lost on the event was the outpouring of support for Bell by her leaders, peers, and friends.

The demonstration of leadership during this period of our service was reflective of emotionally intelligent leaders who understood what people mean to an organization built on and around people.

Her momentary lapses of reason to use illicit drugs despite the addiction were hers; the decisions were wrong and went against the policy, good order, and discipline. However, what did we stand to lose in helping her? This impact asymmetry is consistent with the well-established power of negativity bias in human perception and judgment.

Like Specialist Dean's situation, this one was nuanced. But to paraphrase Dr. Whitt, "*At what risk and the tragedy of abandoning an ally in her time of greatest need did we run if we turned our backs?*"

The intentions behind the gesture were not and will not be known. Frankly, they do not need to be. Often, leaders forget the painful lessons of our impact over our intent. In this instance, the outcome was favorable.

This is not always the case.

I have lived those painful lessons of impact over intent, in which the outcomes can go sideways quickly.

Happily, at least for Bell and me, this instance was life-changing. Like tattoos on the brain, they are always there. I would argue that its impact on Bell's life is still one of the catalysts for her life.

—

The point of making it mandatory for military personnel to subject themselves to inoculations, experimental drugs, and therapeutics[51] has been front-page news and dinner table topics for the past couple of years, more notably since the COVID-19 epidemic.

Historical evidence indicates Kreuger's assertion is warranted, and denying that would be dishonest and careless on my part.

The military has erred in the past.

It will more likely err again. Managing such a large organization is complex, as it's challenging to think that everyone will be happy with every decision. That, too, is a careless assumption. It is significant to recognize that leaders may have to deal with affairs of the heart, which are common occurrences.

I eventually had to.

Matters such as love and marriage.

Should I get a shot or not? These are just some elephant-in-the-room issues that some leaders do not address.

Either ignored blatantly or incidentally, they put your organization at risk. Leaders cannot and should not *hope* these things away. Living precariously on the edge, hoping *it does not occur,* can be a dangerous gamble.

This is just a cautionary reminder that hope is not a course of action.

Historical Context

The National Library of Medicine states that the Department of Defense administers seventeen vaccines, as outlined in the Joint Instruction on Immunizations and Chemoprophylaxis, to prevent infectious diseases among military personnel.

The vaccines are administered to military personnel based on military occupation, the location of the deployment, and mission requirements.[52]

Skeptics about vaccines and their ethical use since the Bosnia and Operation Desert Storm incidents still exist. In 1990, at the request of the Department of Defense, the FDA published an interim rule addressing the DoD's concerns about using products with an Investigational New Drug (IND) status in combat situations.[53]

The interim rule allowed the FDA commissioner to waive the informed consent requirement when such a waiver was requested by the Assistant Secretary of Defense for Health Affairs.

The application of the rule was restricted to the *use* of an investigational drug (including an antibiotic or biological product) in a specific protocol under an Investigational New Drug (IND) application. It was *"limited to a specific military operation involving combat or the immediate threat of combat."*

Coincidentally, the rule was applied during the Gulf War. They allowed the use of pyridostigmine bromide and a botulinum toxoid vaccine to protect against the potential use of weaponized biological or chemical agents.[54]

When service members returned from the Gulf War deployment and reported medically unexplained symptoms, many questioned the safety and efficacy of the vaccine and drug products used during the war and the wisdom of DoD's use of the interim rule.[55]

These beliefs, which may have been different had there been credible evidence of the actual use of chemical or biological weapons, sparked changes in the government's policy.

Because of concerns about using the interim rule during the Gulf War, the U.S. Congress passed an amendment to the Defense Authorization Act for FY 1999 that vests solely with the president the authority to waive the informed consent requirement.[56]

The FDA was again criticized for administering a product with Investigational New Drug (IND) status without closely adhering to its guidelines, as seen in the case of the tick-borne encephalitis (TBE) vaccine. The vaccine, developed by scientists from Austria and the United Kingdom, had been widely used in Europe but had not been licensed in the United States.[57]

There is plenty to be dismissive, curious, and even frightened about here. The underlying reason for the actions was to protect the United States forces serving overseas in hostile areas and countries with deficient medical expertise and care.

—

In my heart, I believe this notion. If not, what are the choices? Not to mention the unknowns of the enemy in using chemical and biological warfare against United States troops.

—

Despite its initial stumble, the military is working to get this right. Military readiness depends on the whole soldier concept, and armchair quarterbacking is easy. The soldier must be physically, medically, mentally, and spiritually ready. There are numerous medical *showstoppers* to deployment. If ignored, it would be reckless and criminal to put unprepared soldiers in harm's way knowingly.

The soldier is also responsible for doing what they can control to stay healthy. Yet, one can do too much in trying to perfect a system through irrational behavior and in haste to suit the immediate status quo. That is why the deliberation that the MDMP and its problem-solving methodology purport to and espouse is effective.

While initially hasty and knee-jerk, the military is still learning from past lessons. They are more adept at addressing the service members' fears. Now, they react quickly to requests for more deliberation in bringing medicines to market and providing complete and truthful information about their safety and efficacy.

They must because their responsibility is to their troops. But it also proves the difficulties Commanders face when confronting the rules and regulatory practices in place when deploying forces into situations that are likely to expose them to infectious disease threats for which licensed vaccines may not be available.[58]

—

Politicians cannot punt their responsibilities in this. They protect the military and the population through prudent law. The brass can and will only speak in one voice at podiums, but informed Americans know what occurs behind the curtains.

You do not have to agree with the stance that service members who refuse vaccines take, but pragmatic, emotionally intelligent leaders do not make excuses for themselves or their teammates; they address them.
Leaders compromise.

They are patient and tolerant, finding common ground by tailoring each situation to a criterion that honors the team. I ask leaders and teammates to pause and reflect on the organization's values and work out what they mean to them individually. Then, they should ask themselves how those values will be recognized and perceived in action and what will happen if they are absent.

Without diminishing anyone's service or what it means to them, remember that sacrifice, though not explicitly worded in your contract, was intended and implied. Sacrifices that no longer only include you. The same incidentally applies to both the private and public sectors. Where there is disagreement with my point of view, and there is.

Those who disagree with my point of view are exercising their beliefs and illuminating the crux and central theme of this book: the ability to see past our insular points of view and exercise the capacity to compromise, problem-solve, and meet goals.

Before moving on, here's a word of caution and a reminder that, along with your daily compromises, individual team members look at themselves in the mirror and remember that *you said you would.*

Your accountability and the effects of decisions on your team are deeply personal discussions you must have with yourself.

—

So, how does this apply to the private and public sectors?

Even two-plus years later, there are still discussions, disagreements, and confusion about the recent COVID-19 epidemic and the question of shots, no shots, booster, no booster, should I go in or stay home, work or not work? The indecisions were plenty.

The early onset of the disease, the unknowns, and the confusion in information sharing and dissemination caused fear and anxiety. Incidents of physical and foul personal attacks on vaccinated and non-vaccinated individuals were reported.

Fear of the unknown is a genuine catalyst. How could the situation have been better handled?

Acting ethically within the systems you create as a leader is paramount and necessary for anyone with a leadership role. Government agencies tasked with finding solutions should have gathered the known facts and truths and informed the nation at a time when they could answer some basic questions without rushing to put out incomplete or unvetted information.

For example, given the available information, a question like *"We know it's dangerous, but is it manageable?"* could have been answered quickly at the outset with more prudence and diligence. However, from my memory, the opposite was true.

I suspect that the fear of the unknown contributed to the confusion. Even though some of the best minds and professionals in the medical world were working diligently, no one wanted to be the last person standing when the *blame game* music ended.

Although there was the appearance of a unified front at the podiums, watch any of the news outlets after the podium appearances, and you can tell there wasn't one. Competent leaders work from the center of gravity and friction points; they do not shy away from them.

Another critical error I observed was that, unlike the military in its decision-making, when the leader and the team have decided, even if there is dissent, everyone speaks in one voice and performs their roles in support of the agreed-upon course of action.

The only exceptions to this paradigm are in the event of ethical and moral improprieties. Then, I expect the more ethically inclined among the teams or groups to take a stand.

I suspect my earlier point would be easier said than done. But in the military, it is expected.

That is because lives are at stake in their decisions. Similarly, it is also valid for the federal government, of which the military is an extension.

The whole must become more significant than the sum of its parts. The military thrives on cooperation. Therefore, it views its teammates as part of the system, not as bystanders to the process.

Leadership that undermines its people removes credibility and breeds distrust, resentment, anger, and fragmented subgroups. This dangerous, resource-intensive phenomenon must be addressed and resolved.

Chapter 9

"Sometimes we make the process more complicated than we need to. We will never make a journey of a thousand miles by fretting about how long it will take or how hard it will be. We make the journey by repeating each day and repeating it repeatedly until we reach our destination."
Joseph B. Wirthlin

Putting it All Together

The most effective leaders share one critical aspect: they all tend to possess exceedingly high degrees of emotional intelligence. Being the best trained, having a sharp analytical mind, being the most astute, and even having an endless supply of brilliant ideas will not make you a great leader without emotional intelligence (EI).

However, those who possess it and some of the other qualities we mentioned are on their way to becoming memorable leaders.

In an environment with numerous options, suggestions, and opinions on issues that affect people, I would only offer that we listen attentively enough to understand the debate. Frame the problem, but frame it correctly. If the problem is framed illogically, you will chase false solutions, wasting personnel hours and resources.

By stating the problem, you are better equipped and able to explore possible solutions. British Prime Minister Margaret Thatcher once said, *"You have to win the debate before you can go out and win the vote."* Similarly, you cannot tackle a problem you have not defined.

You will find that not doing so will waste time, spinning your wheels, because there is no process if you have no point of departure. Consider Sun Tzu's thinking: *"Strategy without tactics is the slowest route to victory, and tactics without strategy are the noise before defeat."*

For you, your idea without execution is your route, and your observation without action is the noise you will hear before failure.

As this book concludes, it provides yet another example of the need for and importance of people. During an interview on CNBC's Squawk Box, Three Arrows Capital Co-Founder Kyle Davis asserted that *"the firm failed partly because of people's involvement!"*[59] He did not attribute the issues to poor business practices on his part and FTX's Sam Bankman-Fried's throughout their transactions.

Seeming not to be outdone, or perhaps due to their conceit or something else not easily explained, in a similar interview with Andrew Ross-Sorkin, [60,] Bankman-Fried
said, *"We completely failed on risks; that feels pretty embarrassing in retrospect."* But don't beat yourself up too much; it was a head-scratcher for most of us, too, given the circumstances, Sam.

Interestingly, they both conducted their interviews remotely to conceal their actual locations.

It begs the question, why? Doesn't it?

With charges now leveled against Bankman-Fried, it will be interesting to see how historians document this. We will all see if, as they say, history is kind.

They could have conceded if it were not for people who, through their oversight and ethical and moral compasses, tempered and rendered their actions less disastrous.

They did not show complicity or take responsibility for their roles.

Instead of equivocating to preserve what was left of their legal rights, as cowardly as that would have been, they both openly spoke. I suspect it was just part of the ego and hubris that are so prominent in white-collar crimes.

Even more interesting, each response was carefully worded and ensured that it included a lot of *we*. Their behaviors indicate their inability to grasp their exploitation of people, some of whom, it was clear, they were ready to throw under the bus and did during the interviews.

This is further evidence that when people are removed from the equation and accountability is removed, the results are single points of failure and corruption. When the culture includes fear, there is inherently indifference and retraction, which causes people to avoid speaking up because they fear reprisals.

But some among us do fight back. Remember Enron? The whistleblower Sherron Watkins' statement to a BBC reporter should give you chills. Watkins was the Vice President of Corporate Development at Enron. She said, *"Blowing the whistle had been like telling the Titanic's captain, we've hit an iceberg, sound the alarm, come up with a plan." Still,* the response was, *"Icebergs don't matter; we're unsinkable."*

I said it should give you chills because such toxic cultures in which peers and other executives spotlight issues and are silenced should beg the question, what about the voice of the factory floor worker? The ones that are not decision-makers?

In the military and through the MDMP, this fear is removed. Arthur Andersen, the Accounting Firm, was contracted to provide consulting and accounting services to Enron in 2001.

At the time, Enron was the 6th largest company in the United States. The business world and anyone paying attention to Business 100 know that businesses, by their name, aim to make a profit. A contract the size of the sixth-largest company is worth winning and keeping; there is no debate about that. But ask yourselves, at what cost?

Unlike Sherron Watkins, Andersen knowingly turned a blind eye. Interestingly, due to the behaviors of Enron and others, new legislation was passed to protect the integrity of the business world and investors.

The Sarbanes-Oxley Act, which states that auditors are barred from providing most, but not all, consulting services to audit clients, was passed in 2002.[61] The relationship between Arthur Andersen and Enron suggests that Enron had Andersen, a member of the *Big Five* accounting firms, in its pocket. Why else would a reputable company put itself at such risk?

If they had chosen to report the wrongdoing, any threat to Andersen would have only highlighted Enron's behavior. Their silence and apathy were complicit behaviors. As the results were later disclosed and discussed earlier in the book, more ego than greed was involved. That does not excuse the behavior.

In retrospect, it makes it scarier. What has shifted in our culture in the past four decades besides greed and power? And the byproducts of industrial and technological growth and progress, which most would embrace and not argue as a negative.

However, the results have escalated over the past few decades with a noticeable increase in white-collar crimes. These crimes are often done at the expense of the less fortunate and others. There are far too many Kenneth Lays, Bernie Madoffs, and now what looks like Bankman-Frieds in private offices and back rooms concocting evil machinations to unleash (often knowingly) on others, all in the name of self-satisfaction and gratification.

There are far too many examples like those mentioned here, making doing nothing about them complicit behavior. An observation not acted upon is just an observation.

People must matter.

It's said that if you see something, say something, and, intrinsically, that's easier said than done, considering the previous discussion. But ask yourself, what are the alternatives?

It should take a significant amount of your time to act in good faith on behalf of people and their importance and value to the systems and processes you develop. People have been and will continue to be the best backstop.

Chapter 10

"The best way out is always through."
Robert Frost

People

Before we close, the military does not have the luxury of selecting those with whom we will work. In the private sector, such opportunities often exist. So, consider these questions when approaching a job and a commitment. Does the makeup of the board, committee, or non-profit make sense?

Is there a noticeable alignment between members and the mission aim of the organization?

Does their expertise provide the *so what?* Finally, will it add value to the boss's and the organization's future vision? You should walk away if the answer to any of these questions is no.

Those are just a few of the significant red flags in poorly led organizations. I hope I have spotlighted enough that you cannot ignore the elephant in the room: our people.

We must embrace all they are and can provide to your corporation and business. So, ask yourself, *"Why doesn't the lion often roar in the jungle?"*

Everyone already knows who it is, and fanfare is not needed. Be confident yet humble.

Be relevant yet obscure where appropriate. Let your teams have their autonomy. Your legacy will not be written by your accomplishments but by your impact on people.

Be an example.

Be fair.

Be frank.

Be honest and keep your integrity. Hearing is an involuntary reaction. Listening is an art.

I often tell my teammates and subordinates that we have two ears and one mouth by design.

Do twice the listening, which also means keeping your mouth closed. If you find that you are formulating your response while hearing what is being spoken, you are not genuinely listening.

You owe this to your teammates and the team.

Processes

People are not machines or inanimate objects.

They feel. They hurt.

They get hot and cold.

They cry.

They marry and raise families.

They smile. They laugh.

People are the catalyst.

It is why Steve Goodier reminds us, *"Who does not want to know that we notice and value them? And who might respond to us better when they feel that they matter? It cannot be overstated – it matters...that people matter."* They are the processes.

The wheels and spokes that keep balance push forward and achieve goals. Like a machine, treat them well. Allow them to get *tuned up.*

Tune them up.

Polish and wax them, and invest time in them, just as you would with the best fuel grade in your performance auto.

Processes are necessary, but more importantly, they are easily understood, traversed, and executed. Remove ambiguity from your operations.

Crosstrain the enterprise where it is proper to capture and retain knowledge. Appoint a knowledge manager. Their duties should include archiving, updating, and issuing instructions on accessing the information they manage.

Encourage collaboration and dialogue. This means you have an *open-door* policy that is genuinely open. Be approachable and thick-skinned.

Ask for and own criticisms of your procedures. That also means refining where prudent and necessary. Remember, an observation not acted upon is just an observation.

Systems

Remember that you legitimize and standardize new behaviors and actions if you are complacent or do not correct missteps. Be cautious when setting new standards. They must be tied to a metric.

They must be measurable.

Make processes as simple as possible.

Do not overwhelm your teams with unnecessary procedures. The fewer steps they take, the more productive they will be. This productivity will explode inward, upward, and outward.

Epilogue

There were a couple of mentions in the book that the Military Decision-Making Process is not a panacea.

It is not.

It cannot be.

Humans are involved and flawed because of our conscious and unconscious nature. Despite that, the Military Decision-Making Process is a blueprint.

A blueprint that depicts how leaders can make better decisions when they remove insularity from their decision-making processes and include the well-intended input of people.

I purposefully left out many stories because they were either too emotional to revisit or too long to keep your attention. The ones I did choose are the most memorable and dear to me. In many ways, they are the instruments of my thinking and who I am.

My twenty years of uniformed service were not all glory years. Every day, I faced personal and professional challenges, which, though I remember the bad ones, have not defined me.

Instead, they gave me agency. I hope you take away the lessons of people's strength in everything we do and the imprints they leave on your legacy and memories.

That includes influential and less influential ones. What should not be lost on you, the reader, is that I have no regrets. Because of leaders like the ones you read about here and emotionally intelligent leadership, I served most of my uniformed service with honorable, good people, some of whom allowed me to develop my leadership skills under their tutelage.

They say always act honorably and uprightly because you never know if you are being emulated. Well, now you know.

The names used in this work are pseudonyms only in print. The impacts and influences left on many of us and countless others extend far beyond words.

Try the methods in your day-to-day life and see what grows from your efforts.

About the Author

Sergeant First Class Warren. S. Pennicooke retired after twenty years of service in the Army, including  four combat tours in Iraq. In addition to Iraq, he served tours in Fort Devens, Massachusetts; Grafenwöhr, Germany; Fort Campbell, Kentucky; Camp Casey, Korea; Fort Knox, Kentucky; and finally, in the 2nd and 3rd brigades of the 25th Infantry Division, Hawaii. He has also held various positions, including Academy Instructor, Observer/Controller, Battle Staff Instructor, Squad Leader, Platoon Sergeant, Operations Non-Commissioned Officer (NCO), Truckmaster, and First Sergeant. His service medals include four Bronze Star Medals, the Meritorious Service Medal, and four Army Commendation Medals. He is a member of the Sergeant Audie Murphy Club. He holds a Graduate Degree in Liberal Studies with a Graduate Certificate in Homeland Security from Thomas Edison State University. Now, he is a military consultant who trains the next generation of Army forces. He is married to Caitlin Pennicooke, DPA., an army officer serving on active duty.

Notes:

1. A Primary Group Analysis.

2. Cohesion and the benefits that solid teams can provide to an organization.

3. Leading change. John Kotter.

4. Ibid., p. 170.

5. J. F. C. Fuller. Military Thinker and Senior British Army Officer.

6. The Foundations of the Science of War. 7. A Swiss psychologist who lived from 1875 to 1961.

8 Stoics: Cleanthes and Panaetius.

9. Heyes C. New thinking: the evolution of human cognition. Philos Trans R Soc Lond.
Biol Sci. 2012 Aug.

10. Evolutionary Psychology has fulfilled an essential function in who we are.

11. Planning and Troop Leading Procedures.

12. Ibid.

13. Hollander, E. P. (2009). Inclusive leadership: The essential leader-follower relationship. New York, NY: Routledge.

14. Favara. L. J. (2009, April 01). ProQuest.
Retrieved from ProQuest.

15. https://www.washingtonpost.com/madeby-history/2022/11/15/ftx-enron-scandal/ 16. Enron's business performance and financial condition during the scandal and bankruptcy.

17. https://www.pbs.org/wgbh/frontline/article/video-clip-boeing-737-max-crashes-fatal-design-flaw-documentary/

18. Harvard Business Review's Katzenbach, Steffen, and Kronley.

19. Culture is not something that can be easily manipulated. Kotter.

20. Culture changes only after you have successfully altered people's actions.

21. nbcnews.com. Imagine the sudden withdrawal of some 18,000 U.S. civilian contractors.

22. Rebels Without a Cause: A New Face of African Warfare.

23. Foreign Affairs.

24. Symbiotic relationships with the governments they nominally oppose.

25. Rebels Without a Cause | Foreign Affairs. https://www.foreignaffairs.com/articles/africa/2022-04-19/rebels-without-cause.

26. The Congolese Rally Democracy is a faction that returned to war.

27. New armed groups led by Army defectors.

28. *Lessons* of Vietnam depend on perspective and interpretation.

29. Commander and Team Guide to Liaison Function.

30. Army Doctrine Publication ADP-5-0 (FM 5-0). Headquarters Department of the Army, Washington, DC, 17 May 2012.

31. Direct, lead, and continuously assess operations 6.

32. Collaboration and dialogue.

33. Lamb, Kyle. Leadership in the Shadows. Trample & Hurdle Publishing, 2014.

34. Each new data they gather is jealously guarded and used for their agenda.

35. The 9/11 Commission Report.

36. https://www.merriam-webster.com/dictionary/culture.

37. Army Doctrine Publication ADP-5-0 (FM 5-0). Headquarters Department of the Army, Washington, DC, 17 May 2012.

38. https://www.merriam-webster.com/dictionary/process.

39. Army Doctrine Publication ADP-5-0 (FM 5-0). Headquarters Department of the Army, Washington, DC, 17 May 2012.

40. Boots on the Ground.

41. An organized framework or method is a set of principles or procedures that govern the way something is done.

42. International Encyclopedia of the Social and Behavioral Sciences (2001). 43. The military is a closed-loop system.

44. International Encyclopedia of the Social and Behavioral Sciences (2001).

45. Rand.org. Center for Military Health Policy Research.

46. The war within. Preventing suicides in the U.S. Military.

47. Religioustolerance.org.

48. Paul Gregory is a research fellow at the Hoover Institution and Cullen Professor Emeritus in the Department of Economics at the University of Houston.

49. Organizations and society.

50. Developing emotionally intelligent leaders is crucial to ethical organizations.

51. A Culture of Inertia.

52. Making it mandatory for military personnel to undergo inoculations, experimental drugs, and therapeutics.
53. National Library of Medicine.
54. Department of Defense.
55. National Library of Medicine. Potential use of weaponized biological or chemical agents.
56. The wisdom of DoD's use of the interim rule.
57. The Authorization Act for FY 1999 vests solely with the President the authority to waive the informed consent requirement.
58. The vaccine, developed by scientists from Austria and the United Kingdom, had been widely used in Europe but had not been licensed in the United States.
59. CNBC's Squawk Box.
60. Deal Book Conference.
61. The Sarbanes Oxley Act.
62. www.hg.org

References:

(Various), L. (2023, January 31). *The Fallout of Arthur Andersen and Enron on the Legal Landscape of American Accounting*. Retrieved from hg.org: https://www.hg.org/legal-articles/the-fallout-of-arthur-andersen-and-enron-on-the-legal-landscape-of-american-accounting-31277

Bankman-Fried, S. (2022, November 30). The collapse of FTX. (A. Ross-Sorkin, Interviewer)

Burns, R., Acosta, J., Jaycox, L., & Ramchand, R. (2011). *The War Within: Preventing Suicide in the U.S. Military*. Santa Monica: RAND. Center for Military Health Policy Research.

Burroughs, T. J., & Ruth, S. G. (2022). Cohesion in the Army: A Primary Group Analysis. *Military Review: The Professional Journal Of the U.S. Army*, 11.

Chan, D. (2011, October 9). *Perceptions of Fairness: The perceived fairness of process and treatment is as significant as outcomes when engaging employees, stakeholders, or the public*. Retrieved from csc.gov.sg: https://www.csc.gov.sg/articles/perceptions-of-fairness

Chelaney, B. (2021, August 30). Biden's handling of the Afghanistan situation is a disaster. *Nikkei Asia*.

Curwen, L. (2021, August 3). The Collapse of Enron and the Dark Side of Business. *BBC News: Business*. Davis, K. (2022, November 16) Three Arrow Capital's claims against FTX. (K. Rooney, Interviewer)

Day, D., Gronn, P., & Salas, E. (2004). Leadership Ca-
    pacity in Teams. *The Leadership Quarterly*, pp. 857-
    880.

Dictionary, M.-W. (2022). *Merriam-Webster Diction-
    ary*.

Favara, L. F. (2009, April 1). *Examining followership
    styles and their relationship with job satisfaction and
    performance.* Retrieved from ProQuest.com:
    https://www.proquest.com/docview/305167
    384/fulltextPDF/74FE5DC9D3AA4F39PQ/3? ac-
    countid=40921

Fuller, J. (1993). *The Foundations of the Science of War.*
    Fort Leavenworth: A Military Classic Reprint: U.S
    Army Command and General Staff College Press.

Gregory, P. (2010). Ethical Leadership. *Training Jour-
    nal*, 5.

Hanselman, S. (2022, October 6). *The 9 Core Stoic Be-
    liefs*. Retrieved from Daily Stoic: https://dai-
    lystoic.com/9-core-stoic-beliefs/

Hayes, J. (2014). *The Theory and Practice of Change
Management.* New York: Palgrave Macmillan.

HEADQUARTERS, D. O. (2019). *The Operations Pro-
    cess: ADP-5-0.*

Heard, F. C. (2019). Planning and Troop Leading
    Procedures. *Non-Commissioned-Officer Journal.*

Heyes, C. (2012, August 5). *National Library of Medi-
    cine.* Retrieved from
    www.ncbi.nlm.nih.gov: https://Hanselman, S.
    (2022, October 6).

The 9 Core Stoic Beliefs. Retrieved from Daily Stoic:
    https://dailystoic.com/9-core-stoic-beliefs/

Hayes, J. (2014). *The Theory and Practice of Change
    Management.* New York: Palgrave Macmillan.

Hollander, E. (2009). *Inclusive Leadership: The*

Essential Leader-Follower-Relationship. New York: Rutledge. Retrieved from Hollander, E. P. (2009). Inclusive leadership: The essential leader-follower

Jaycox, L., Acosta, J., Burns, R., Pernin, C., & Ramchand, R. (2011). *The War Within: Preventing Suicides in the U.S Military.* Santa Monica: RAND Center for Military Health Policy Research.

Katzenbach, J. R., Steffen, I., & Kronley, C. (2012, August). www.ncbi.nlm.nih.gov/pmc/arti-cles/PMC3385676/

Kean, Thomas. H; Hamilton, Lee. H; Ben-Veniste, Richard; Kerry, Bob; Fielding, Fred. F; Lehman, John. F; from www.ncbi.nlm.nih.gov: https://www.ncbi.nlm.nih.gov/pmc/arti-cles/PMC338567/

Kearns, J. K. (2022). Rebels Without a Cause: A New Face of African Warfare. *Foreign Affairs.*

Kotter, J. P. (2012). *Leading Change.* Boston: Harvard Business Review Press.

Krueger, G. (2001). The Military as a Social Psychological Experimental Proving Ground. *International Encyclopedia of the Social Sciences.*

Learned, C. F. (2022). *20-05-Commander and Staff Guide to Liaison Function.* Center for Army Lessons Learned.

Learned, C. F. (2022, October 9). *Military Decision-Making Process (MDMP): Lessons and Best Practices.* Retrieved from https://cgsc.contentdm.oclc.org/: https://cgsc.contentdm.oclc.org/digital/collec-tion/p15040coll4/id/46/

Pollack, K. M. (2022). The Middle East Abhors a Vacuum: America's Exit and the Coming Contest for Military Supremacy. *Foreign Affairs.*

SGM Lamb, K. (2014). *Leadership in the Shadows.* Nashville: Trample & Hurdle.

Taddonio, P. (2021, September 14). In 737 Max Crashes, Boeing Pointed to Pilot Error — Despite a Fatal Design Flaw. *Frontline.*

Whitt, J. (2019, October 28). *War Room – U.S. Army War College Creative Thinking about National Security and Defense.* Retrieved from war-room.armywarcollege.edu: https://war-room.armywarcollege.edu/special-series/whiteboard/wb10-legacy-of-vietnam/

Zinsmeister, K. (2003). *Boots on the Ground: A Month with the 82nd Airborne in the Battle for Iraq.* New York: Martin's Press.